MELODIC CELLS FOR JAZZ GUITAR

The Quickest Way to Master Tension, Resolution & Phrasing on Jazz Guitar

OZ NOY

With Tim Pettingale

FUNDAMENTAL CHANGES

Melodic Cells for Jazz Guitar

The Quickest Way to Master Tension, Resolution & Phrasing on Jazz Guitar

ISBN: 978-1-78933-385-5

Published by www.fundamental-changes.com

Copyright © 2022 Oz Noy

With Tim Pettingale

The moral right of this author has been asserted.

All rights reserved. No part of this publication may be reproduced, stored in a retrieval system, or transmitted in any form or by any means, without the prior permission in writing from the publisher.

The publisher is not responsible for websites (or their content) that are not owned by the publisher.

www.fundamental-changes.com

Over 13,000 fans on Facebook: **FundamentalChangesInGuitar**

Instagram: **FundamentalChanges**

For over 350 Free Guitar Lessons with Videos Check Out

www.fundamental-changes.com

Cover Image Copyright: Author photo by Yossi Zwecker, used by permission

Contents

About the Author 4

Introduction 5

Get the Audio 7

Chapter One – Mixolydian Scale Cells 8

Chapter Two – Whole Tone Scale Cells 23

Chapter Three – Diminished Scale Cells 48

Chapter Four – Altered Scale Cells 75

Conclusion 99

About the Author

Born in Israel, Oz started his professional career at the age of 13 playing jazz, blues, pop and rock music. By age 16, he was playing with top Israeli musicians and artists. At 24, he was one of the most established guitar players in the country. Oz was also a member of the house band on Israel's top-rated television show for more than two years.

Since his arrival in New York in 1996, Oz has made a huge impact on the local and international music scene. His unique, intoxicating style has broken all the rules of instrumental guitar music by focusing on the groove. Renowned drummers Keith Carlock, Anton Fig, Vinnie Colaiuta, Steve Ferrone, Chris Layton, Dennis Chambers and Dave Weckl have contributed to his recordings, as well as all-star bassists Will Lee, James Genus, John Patitucci, Roscoe Beck and Reggie Washington.

Oz is a prolific recording artist, releasing his debut record, *Oz Live*, in 2001, recorded at NYC's legendary Bitter End. Since then, highlights have included his highly acclaimed studio record, *HA!* with an all-star band featuring Fig, Carlock, Lee and Genus, plus special guests Mike Stern and George Whitty; the 2009 release, *Schizophrenic*, featuring special guest Steve Lukather; *Twisted Blues Vol.1* and *Vol.2*, featuring guests including John Medeski, Eric Johnson, Allen Toussaint, Chic Corea and Warren Haynes; and *Who Gives a Funk?* featuring Joe Bonamassa, Robben Ford, Dweezil Zappa, Fred Wesley, Chris Potter, John Medeski and Corey Glover.

In 2019 Oz released his Boogaloo-inspired album *Booga Looga Loo* and in 2020 released *Snapdragon*, exploring new sonic territory and with guests including Dennis Chambers, Will Lee, Vinnie Colaiuta, Dave Weckl, James Genus, and John Patitiucci and Chris Potter.

For his accomplishments as a trend-setting guitarist, Oz won the highly acclaimed *Guitar Player* magazine readers' poll for "Best guitar riff on a record" (2007), "Best new talent" (2008), and "Best out-there guitar player" (2013).

Oz's success as an artist and instrumentalist has created a demand for him as a teacher. He has released two instructional videos for Jazz Heaven, *Guitar Improvisational Workout* and *Play Along Workout*, and three videos for My Music Master Class entitled *Unlocking the Neck, Blues, Bends and Beyond* and *Effects on the Gig*. He has also created four video courses for TrueFire: *Twisted Guitar: Blues Soloing, Twisted Guitar: Blues Rhythm, Essentials: Funk Rhythm Guitar* and *Improv Wizard*. Oz conducts occasional master classes at The Collective School of Music (New York City), Musicians Institute (Los Angeles), and others.

Oz has toured and recorded with too many artists to name them all here! Highlights include: Chris Botti, Cyndi Lauper, Toni Braxton, Nile Rodgers, Roger Glover, Warren Hayes, The Allman Brothers, Allen Toussaint, Eric Johnson, Mike Stern, John Abercrombie, Steve Lukather, Richard Bona, Gavin Degraw, Nelly Furtado, Natasha Bedingfield, Jennifer Hudson, Don Henley, Patti Austin, Take 6, Michael Bublé, Josh Groban, Phil Ramone, Dweezil Zappa, Steven Tyler, Joe Perry, Sting, Steve Perry, Allison Krauss, Foreigner, Patty Smyth, Idina Menzel, Justin Timberlake, Bonnie Raitt and Dave Mathews.

Introduction

Over the years, I've taught hundreds of guitar players, and during that time I've noticed a recurring theme. Whenever I work with students who are interested in improving their modern jazz guitar playing, it's always how they navigate the V to I chord resolution that lets them down.

You don't have to play jazz for very long to understand that the Major and Minor ii V I chord progressions are the most important sequences to learn to solo over. They occur in every single jazz standard, apart from certain modal tunes. Master the ii V I and, in theory, you've done most of the hard work needed to be a competent jazz player. But here's the thing…

I've sat with many players who can blow over the ii V I sequence, yet there's still a weakness to the lines they play. The problem is not moving from the ii to the V chord, it's resolving the V chord to the I. Many people play lines that resolve awkwardly, or don't resolve at all. You still don't get the sense that the line has returned "home". We can add to this, the fact that many players' phrasing leaves a lot to be desired.

So, I devised a method that would, first of all, teach people how to structure great sounding licks that resolve in a musically satisfying way and, secondly, that would open up their ears to exciting altered sounds over the V chord *before* reaching that resolution. The results I've seen from students who have worked through this approach have been quite phenomenal. So much so, that together with my publisher, Fundamental Changes, we thought it was worth putting the method into the book you hold in your hands.

Here's how I set about tackling the problem and what to expect from this book.

Phrasing is one of the most difficult things to master on guitar. We tend to learn guitar very differently than, say, piano or saxophone, and it's easy to play a lot of notes on guitar without really saying much. So, in this book you'll find a comprehensive library of succinct, well-formed phrases that perfectly resolve from chord V to chord I. I call them *melodic cells* because that's literally what they are: small cellular ideas that can be used to connect other ideas together in a coherent, stable manner.

Learn these melodic cells and you'll discover two things:

First, your phrasing will improve immediately. Discipline yourself to play well-formed ideas again and again, and good phrasing will be the natural byproduct.

Second, your vocabulary will grow. Learning melodic cells is like learning a new word every day from a language you're studying. Repetition helps to embed these new ideas and, before you know it, you're using them without thinking.

If I were to add a third benefit, it's that you'll be inspired with new ideas. I've seen the musical growth of students who've seriously applied this method and noticed how they spontaneously play more creative lines – lines they wouldn't have thought to play before. Once this method starts to soak in, it will improve your all-round musicianship.

Each chapter in this book follows the same format. Remember that the focus is on how we resolve from the V chord to the I chord.

Chapter One covers the Mixolydian scale – the go-to scale for many because it perfectly fits the dominant V chord. Here's how we will work with it:

- First, you'll learn 4 melodic 1/8th note cells. These are melodic lines built from the four chord tones that make up the dominant chord (root, 3rd, 5th, b7)

- Next, you'll learn a couple of relatively simple ii V I, 1/8th note licks for each of the four cells, to help embed the idea

- Then, you'll work through a collection of licks built using each of the four cells. Four cells might not sound like much, but double them by playing them in two octaves, and surround them by other ideas and the melodic possibilities are endless. These licks will teach you to apply more creativity to your line construction, breaking things up rhythmically and thinking more intervallically. There are lots of cool licks here for you to add to your vocabulary

Chapters two to four are where things really hot up, as we apply the exact same formula to some exotic scales. We'll repeat the process using the Whole Tone, Half-Whole Diminished and Altered scales as the source of our melodic cells. The result is some really fresh sounding, modern melodic jazz lines you can use to further extend your jazz vocabulary.

Altogether, this book is a complete resource for the jazz guitarist who wants to break out of a rut and elevate their melodic knowledge and phrasing. However, if you really want to get the most out of this method long term, then also check out my first book, *Inside-Outside Guitar Soloing*. It contains tons of exercises to help you master the Mixolydian and altered scales in a structured manner, as well as demonstrating how to use them practically to create licks and solos.

Enjoy the journey!

Oz

Get the Audio

The audio files for this book are available to download for free from **www.fundamental-changes.com.** The link is in the top right-hand corner. Click on the "Guitar" link then simply select this book title from the drop-down menu and follow the instructions to get the audio.

We recommend that you download the files directly to your computer, not to your tablet, and extract them there before adding them to your media library. You can then put them onto your tablet, iPod or burn them to CD. On the download page there are instructions and we also provide technical support via the contact form.

For over 350 free guitar lessons with videos check out:

www.fundamental-changes.com

Over 13,000 fans on Facebook: **FundamentalChangesInGuitar**

Tag us for a share on Instagram: **FundamentalChanges**

Chapter One – Mixolydian Scale Cells

We're going to learn the cellular approach by working with the Mixolydian scale. It's the most "inside" sounding of the scales we'll work with, but it's the go-to scale for many jazz musicians because it perfectly spells the sound of the dominant 7 chord.

It's an important scale to know, because in the ii V I sequence that forms the backbone of jazz, the ii chord is often ignored in favor of the V chord. In jazz thinking, the ii and the V are the same sound, but the V chord is the important focal point because it has the potential to be altered, and therefore allows us to play more interesting scales over it. We'll get to those scales in subsequent chapters, but the Mixolydian should not be overlooked – when used creatively, we can make some really great music with it.

The G Mixolydian scale

G Mixolydian is the fifth mode in the key of C Major and fits perfectly over a G7 chord, which contains the notes G B D F. The table below shows the notes of the scale and its intervals.

G	A	B	C	D	E	F
Root	2nd	3rd	4th	5th	6th	b7

The scale has the same notes as its C Major parent scale, so some guitarists interpret it as a C Major scale that begins and ends on the note G. However, it's much better to learn G Mixolydian as a scale and (more importantly) a *sound* in its own right.

Scale shapes

Below the G Mixolydian scale is illustrated in two positions, with root notes on the sixth and fifth strings.

The chord grids indicate the location of the root notes, so you can easily transpose the scale to other keys. I nearly always use these three-note-per-string scale patterns, as I find this the easiest way to access the scale and navigate the full range of the fretboard.

The first pattern is the sixth string root shape, which begins on the G note on the 3rd fret.

G Mixolydian

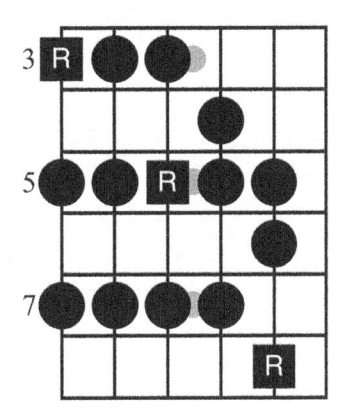

And here is the fifth string root shape, beginning on the 10th fret.

G Mixolydian

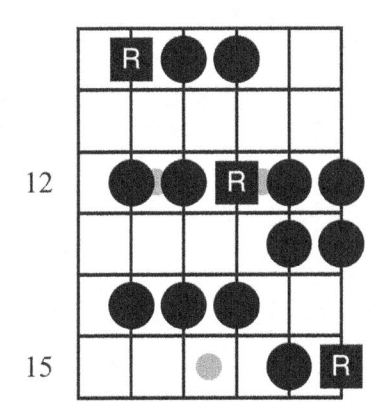

For a structured method to learn this scale and master it across the fretboard, refer to my book *Inside-Outside Guitar Soloing* by Fundamental Changes.

Now we're going to take the chord tones of G7 (G B D F) and use the Mixolydian scale to build 4 melodic cells – one from each chord tone. Each melodic line will outline the G7 chord, then resolve to the I chord (Cmaj7). Let's hear how they sound.

The melodic cells

First, here is the Mixolydian scale played from the root note of G7, resolving to Cmaj7. The cell is played in two octaves. The sound should be familiar to you, as it's a stock phrase that has been used by many great jazz guitarists, but we'll soon be using it to cover some new territory.

Example 1a – Cell 1

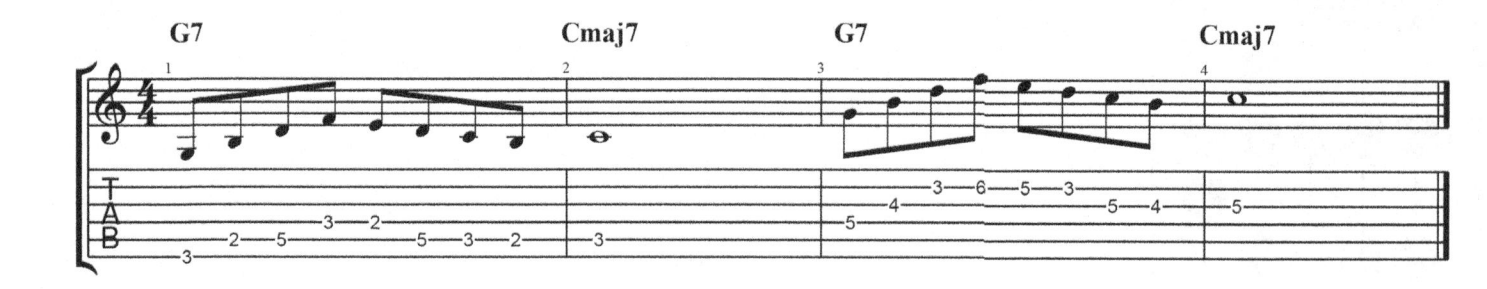

The second cell uses the same phrasing, but this time we play the Mixolydian scale from the 3rd (B) of G7.

Example 1b – Cell 2

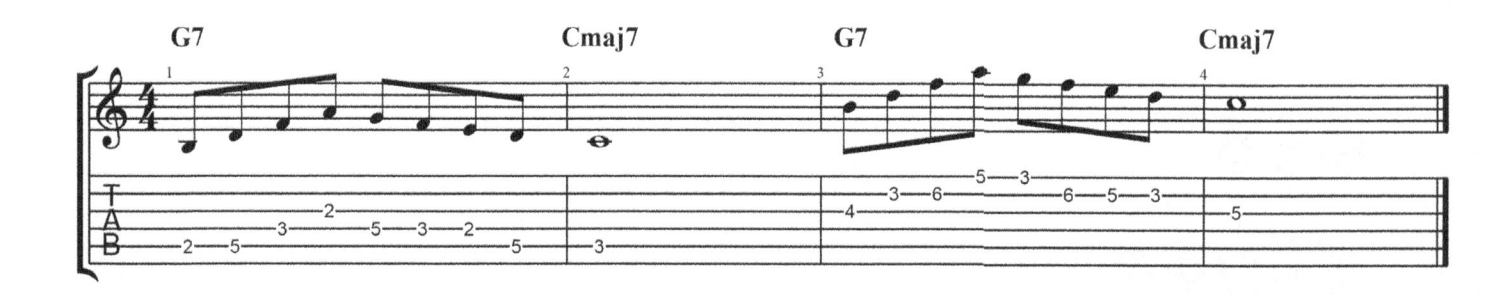

Now let's play a similar line from the 5th (D). Notice that we resolve to a different chord tone of Cmaj7 this time. Wherever the cell ends, we can choose to resolve to a I chord note that is within easy reach.

Example 1c – Cell 3

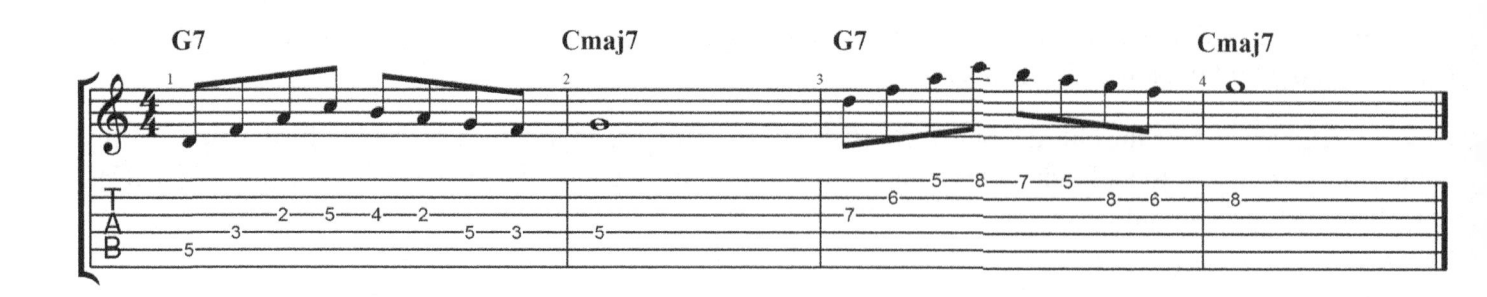

And finally, from the b7 (F).

Example 1d – Cell 4

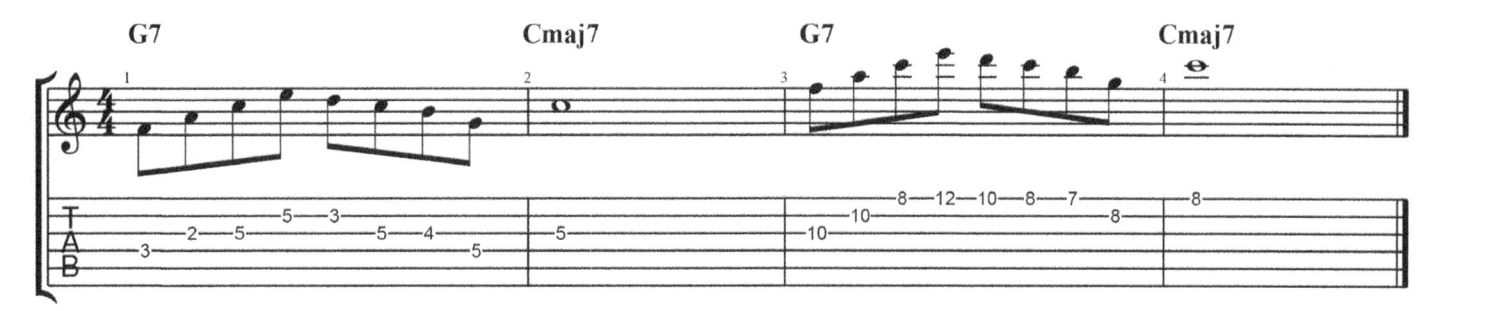

These four cells are our four basic building blocks. From them flow all the melodic ideas in the remainder of this chapter.

Play each one several times and get used to launching the line from each chord tone. Developing the ability to play a scale from any dominant 7 chord tone is going to be a key skill for your future playing. Learn these four cells inside out, in both octaves, until the shape of them is embedded in muscle memory. Aim to reach the place where playing them is completely automatic.

Putting the cells into a Major ii V I

Now that we have the melodic cells in place, let's practice using them in complete jazz lines that span the Major ii V I progression in C Major. We'll start with two simple lines for each cell.

Later, we'll vary the rhythm and phrasing to make more interesting lines, but right now we're still embedding the sound and the playing approach.

We'll start with Cell 1 – the Mixolydian scale played from the root note of G7.

Over the ii chord (Dm7) we can play any kind of G Mixolydian scale-based phrase that occurs to us, but over the V chord (G7) we'll play Cell 1, exactly as demonstrated in Example 1a. Here's how that sounds.

Example 1e

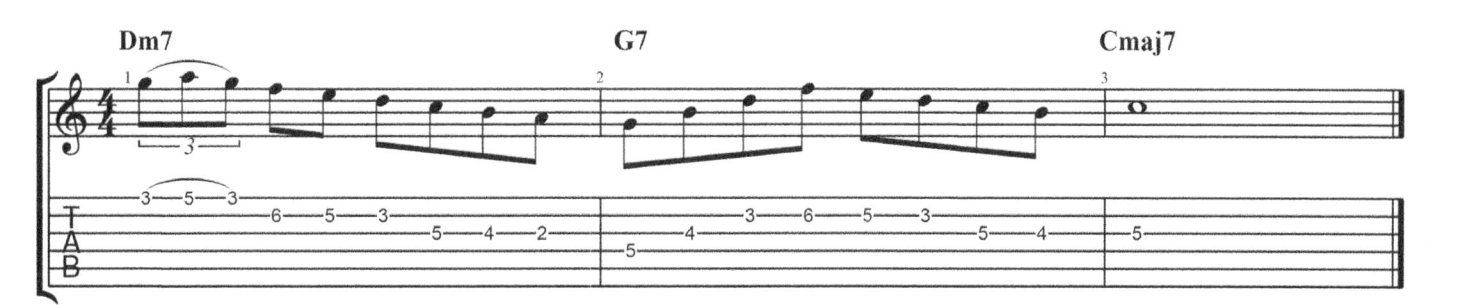

Let's try another line using Cell 1. This time I played a different line in bar one, but the cell appears in bar two, note for note. Notice that because the phrase in bar one has been varied, the cell doesn't sound boring, it just resolves nicely to the root of the C Major chord.

Example 1f

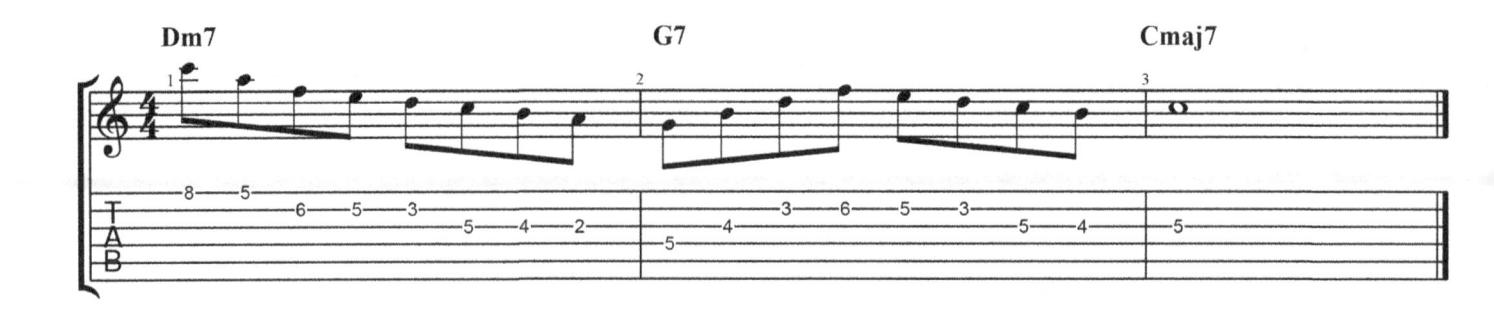

Now let's move on to Cell 2 – the Mixolydian scale played from the 3rd (B) of G7.

Here's the first lick using that cell in bar two. The beauty of this cellular approach is that no matter what we play around it, the cell *anchors* the line and gives it the stability that is so often missing from musicians' playing.

Example 1g

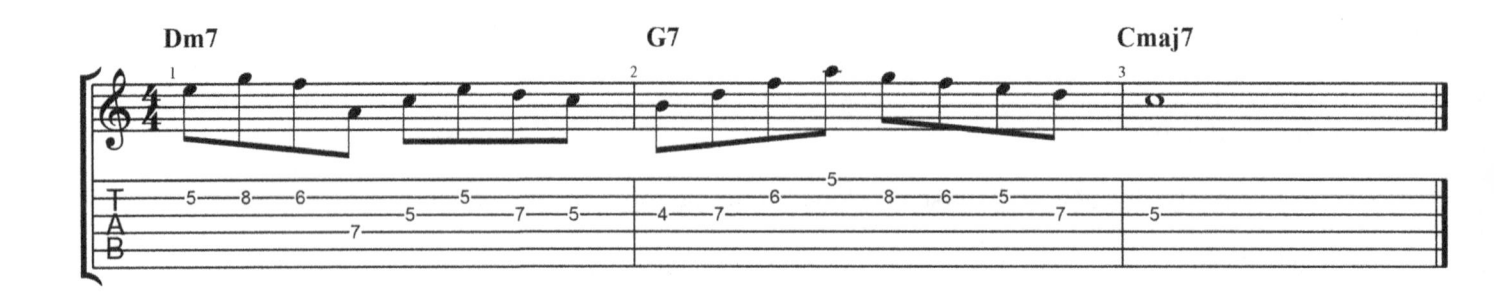

Here's another line that uses Cell 2.

Example 1h

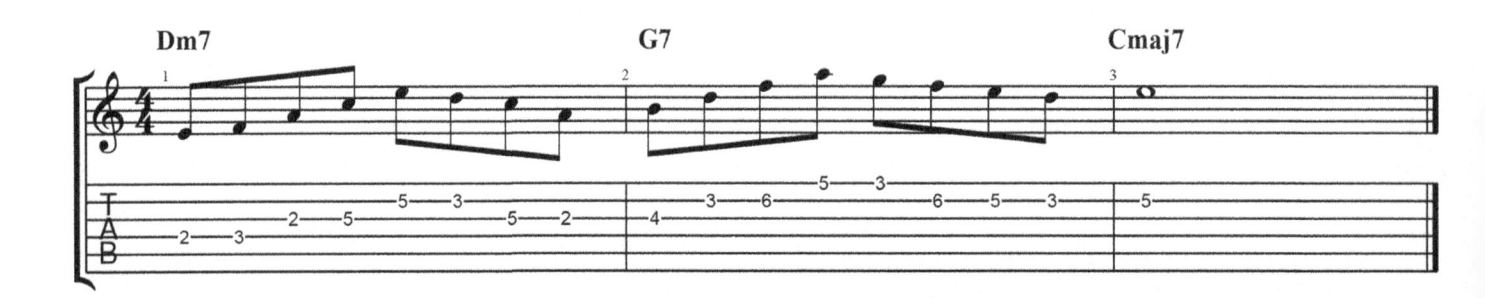

Next, here are two lines that incorporate Cell 3 – the Mixolydian scale played from the 5th (D) of G7.

Notice that for these lines, it made sense to resolve to a different chord tone of Cmaj7. On the second string, the 3rd (E) and 5th (G) of Cmaj7 are both within easy reach, so resolving to one of them makes for a smoother line.

Example 1i

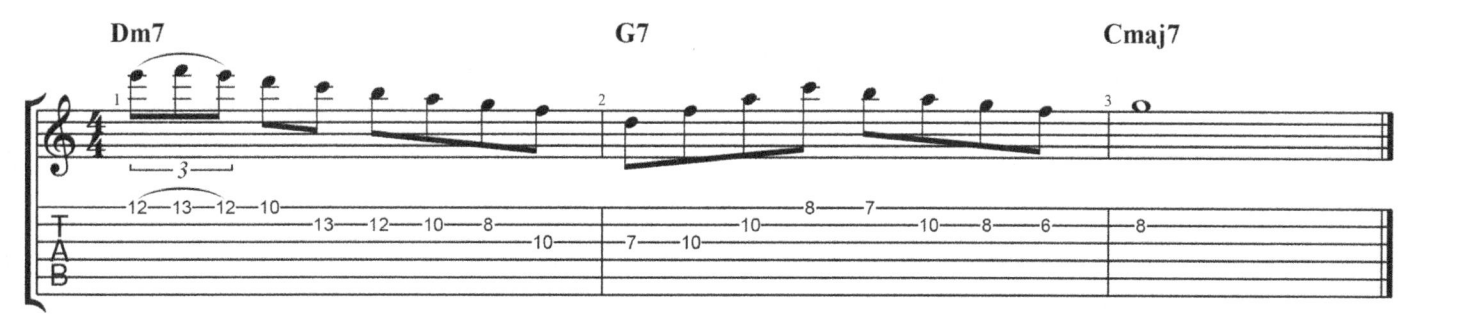

Here's another line using Cell 3, resolving to the 5th of Cmaj7.

Example 1j

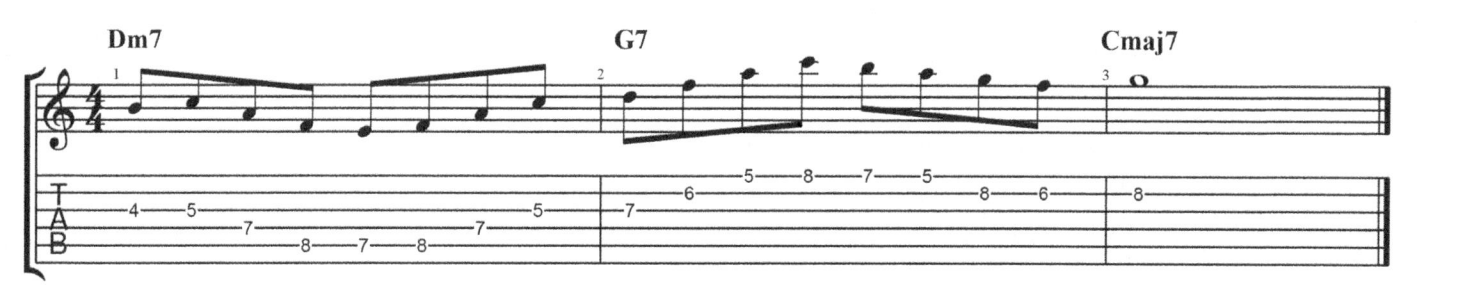

Lastly, here are two lines that use Cell 4 – the Mixolydian scale played from the b7 (F) of G7. For these ideas, it sounds cool to resolve to the root of Cmaj7 using a 4th interval movement. Here's the first:

Example 1k

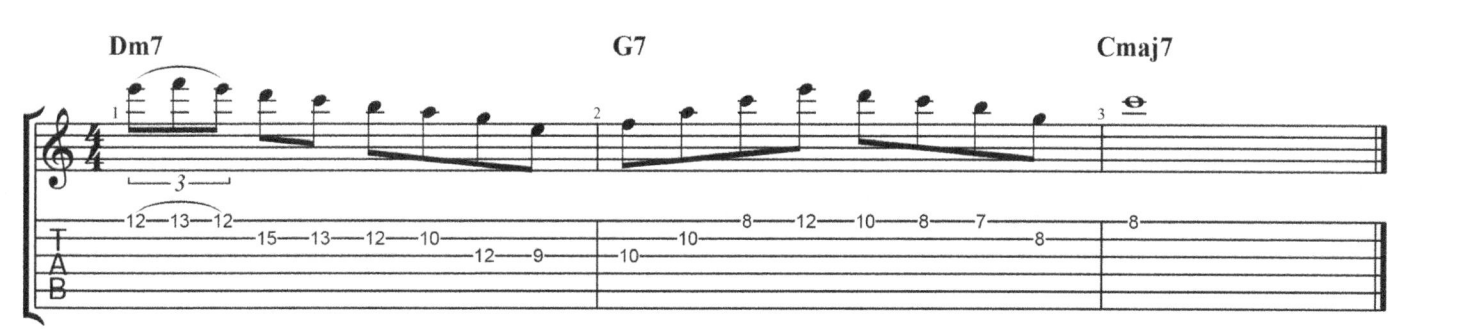

And here's a different approach.

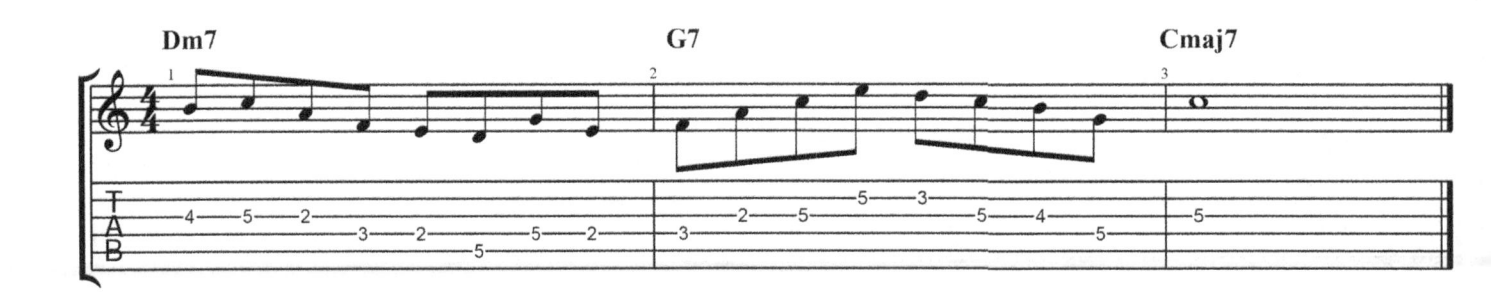

Example 1l

More advanced cellular vocabulary

Let's pause for a review. So far, we've played a series of cellular ii V I's that clearly define the sound of the dominant 7 chord, have a very stable sound, and resolve smoothly to the I chord.

Now it's time to make our lines more creative by adding rhythmic variation. As you'll see in the examples that follow, we can achieve this in a number of ways:

- We can break up the rhythm of the line in bars one and three, leaving the cell intact
- We can vary the rhythm of the cell itself
- We can do both
- We can make the phrases surrounding the cell more intervallic
- We can split lines between octaves
- We can introduce occasional chromatic passing notes

Really, the possibilities are endless limited only by our imagination. What's important is that we retain the *shape* of the cellular idea in bar two, so that we get the smooth V to I chord resolution we're aiming for.

In this section there are five lines for each of the four cells, each using phrasing in different ways to produce more interesting lines. You can add these lines straight into your jazz vocabulary and know that they'll work perfectly every time.

We're working in C Major here, but now that you understand the concept behind creating these lines, you should transpose them to other keys and test them out over your favorite standards.

First, here are five lines that use Cell 1 – the Mixolydian from the root note of G7.

In this first example, the cell remains intact but the rhythm in bar one is broken up with an 1/8th note triplet. One passing note is played as part of an enclosure that targets the F note that falls on beat 3 of bar one (the b7 of G7).

Example 1m

This line uses 1/8th note triplets throughout to vary the rhythm, including in the cell. At the end of bar one, the Ab passing note is targeting the root note of G7 on beat 1 of bar two.

Example 1n

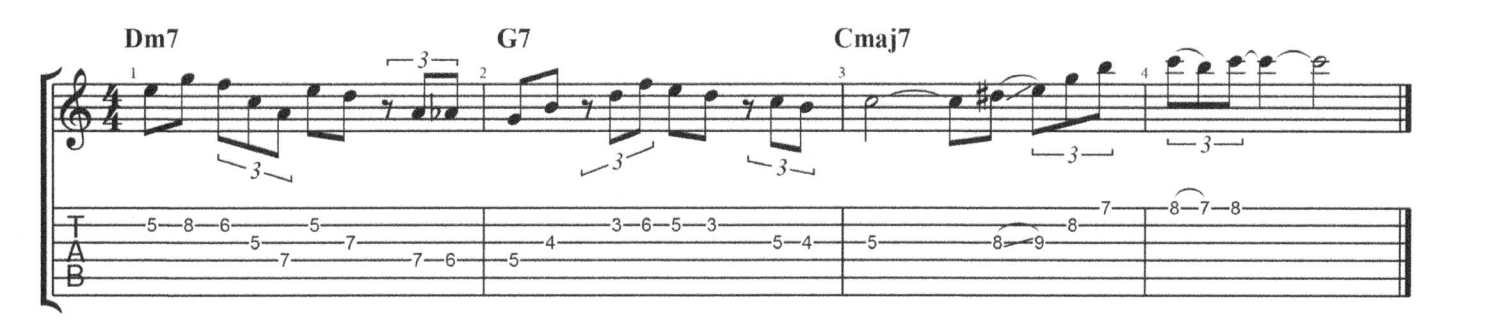

Example 1o uses a question and answer approach, where the phrasing of bar one is replicated in bar two.

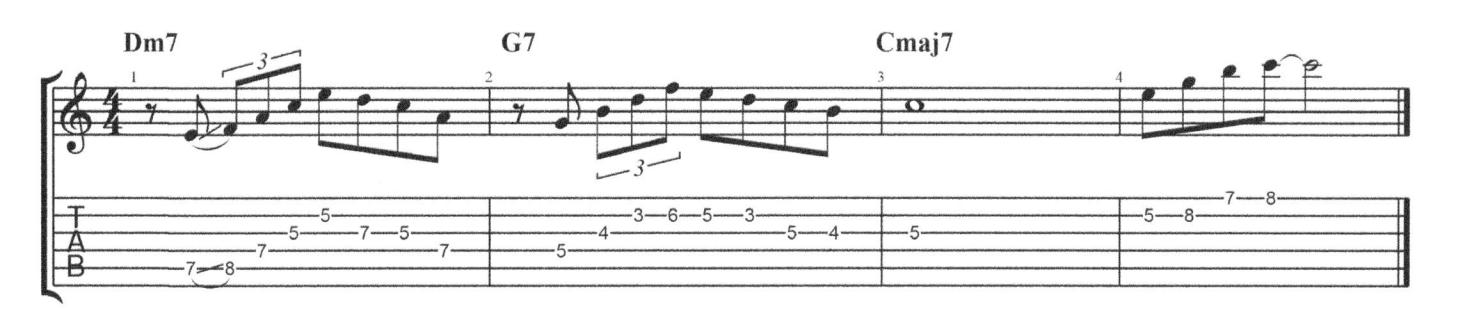

Example 1o

Here's an idea that keeps the G7 cell intact but breaks up the scalic ideas with some intervallic jumps for a more contemporary sound.

Example 1p

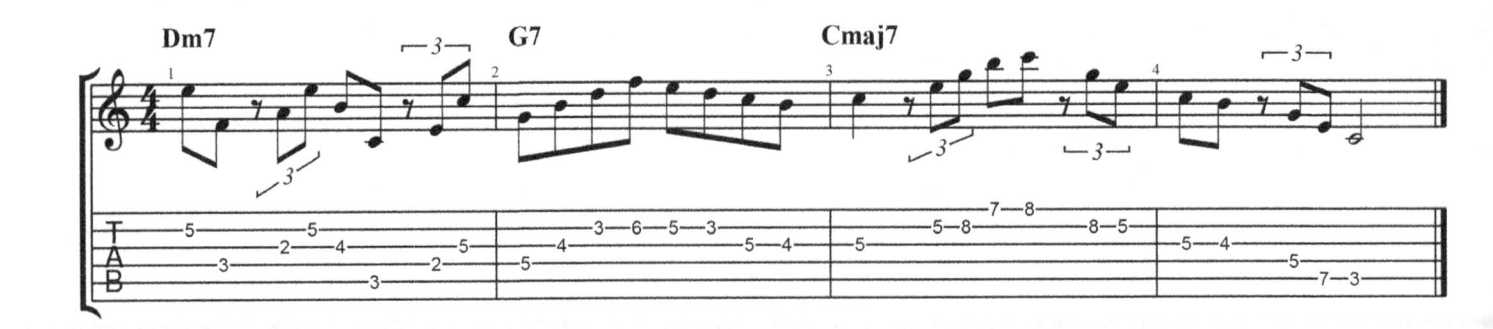

Here's a different intervallic take on the previous line.

Example 1q

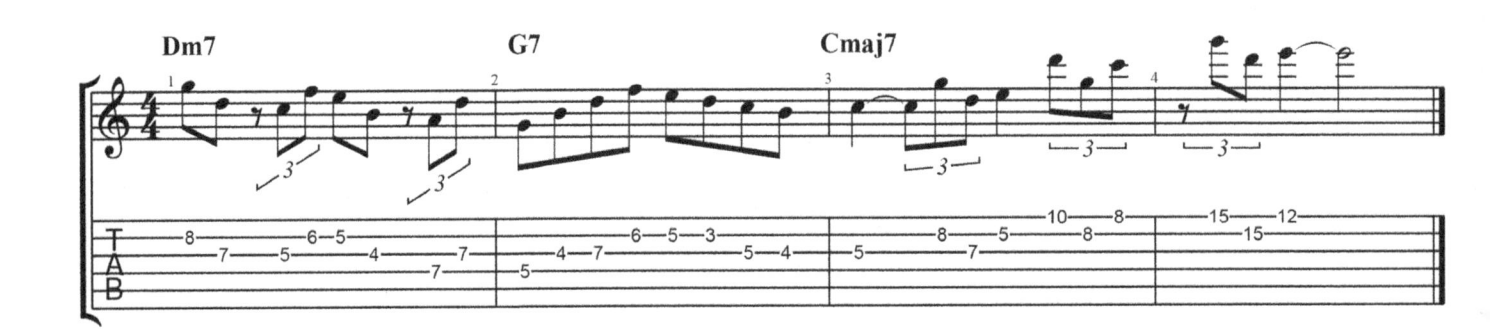

Now we move on to play five lines that use Cell 2 – the Mixolydian from the 3rd of G7.

Our first example uses some Joe Pass style triplet articulations to create rhythmic interest.

Example 1r

Example 1s uses a call and response phrasing idea in bars 1-2, with an 1/8th note rest "interrupting" the response phrase in bar two, just to break up the rhythm of the line some more. Then, an intervallic sequence spells out the Cmaj7 chord.

Example 1s

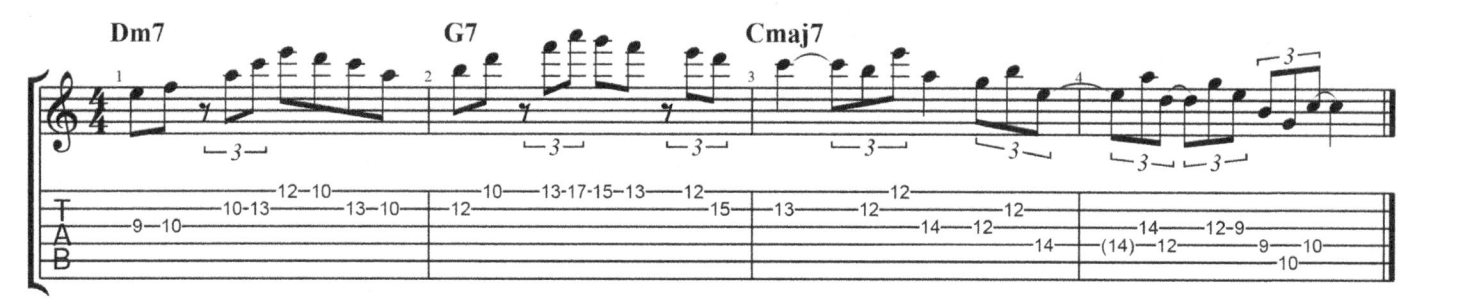

In the next example, the five-note phrase that opens the line is a rhythmic surprise that helps us to avoid playing clichéd patterns. The phrasing of the cell in bar two avoids playing notes on beats 1 and 3, which further helps to break up the rhythm.

Example 1t

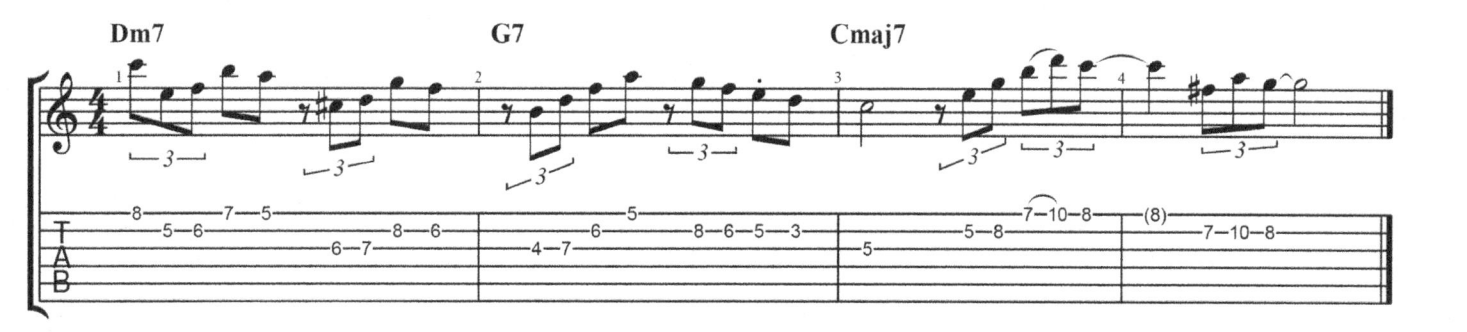

For some harmonic variety, the next line begins on a surprise chromatic passing note. It's an enclosure idea, where the D# and Gb notes target the F scale tone, then the D# note is used again to approach the E scale tone. Having played this outside sounding line in bar one, playing the cell normally in bar two really grounds the line in the harmony once again.

Example 1u

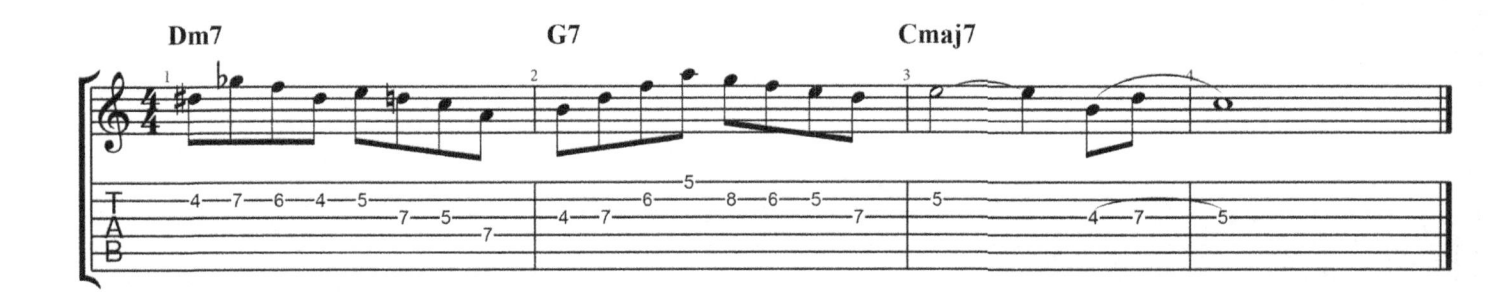

The final Cell 2 example uses string skips in bar one to produce some wide intervals. The string jumps can be tricky to execute cleanly, so play this one slowly to begin with and work out a good economical fingering that you find comfortable. In bar two, the cell is played straight, and an intervallic phrase is played over the Cmaj7.

Example 1v

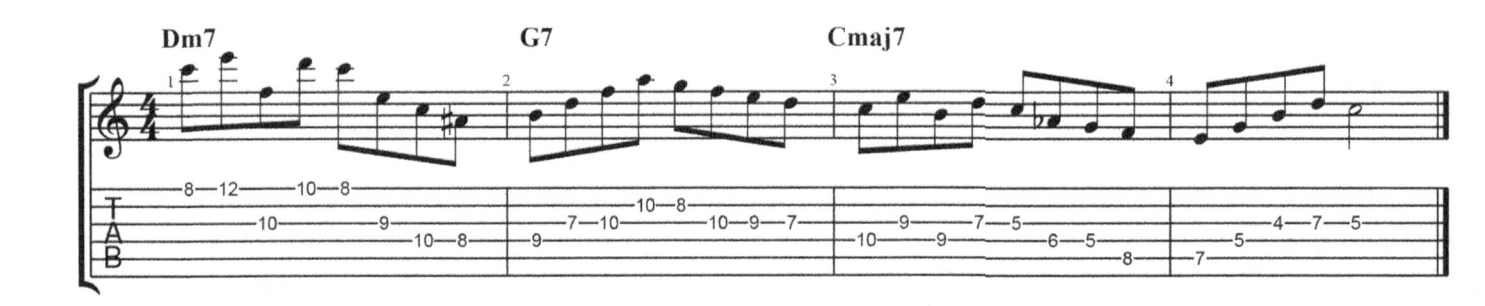

Now let's explore five lines that use Cell 3 – the Mixolydian from the 5th of G7.

To kick things off, here's the most outside sounding line we've played so far. The line begins with a C note, the 4th degree of the G Mixolydian scale, which is followed by a series of chromatic notes in bar one. The idea here is to "side step" the scale down a half step. All of the flat notes in bar one are G Mixolydian scale tones shifted down a half step. There is one more scale tone in the phrase (the F that falls on beat 3), but this just occurs naturally as part of the shape I played.

Notice that bar one creates a lot of tension but the cellular idea in bar two quickly resolves this to ground the harmony.

Example 1w

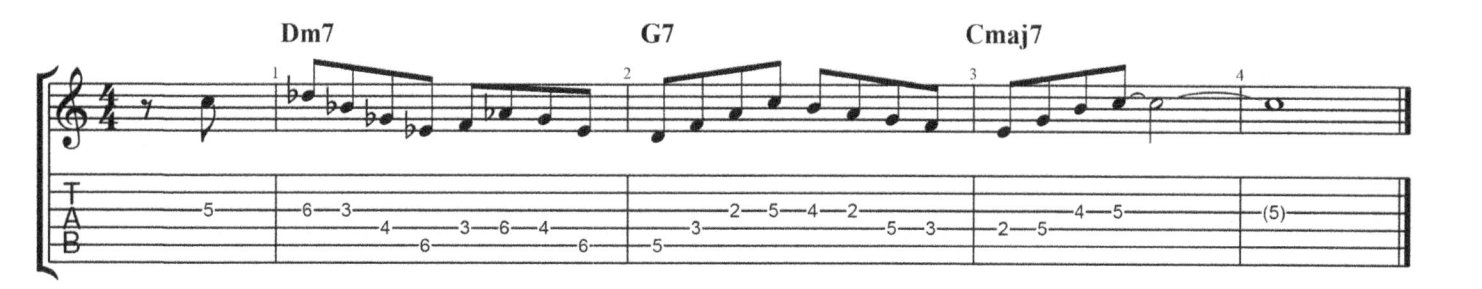

Here's another line that uses a passing note idea. First, an unexpected G# note falls on the 3& of bar one. The two-note phrase that follows is a side step movement that approaches the G7 chords at the beginning of bar two from a half step above.

Example 1x

The next example is a straighter swinging line that uses just one chromatic approach note to lead into the cell in bar two from a half step below.

Example 1y

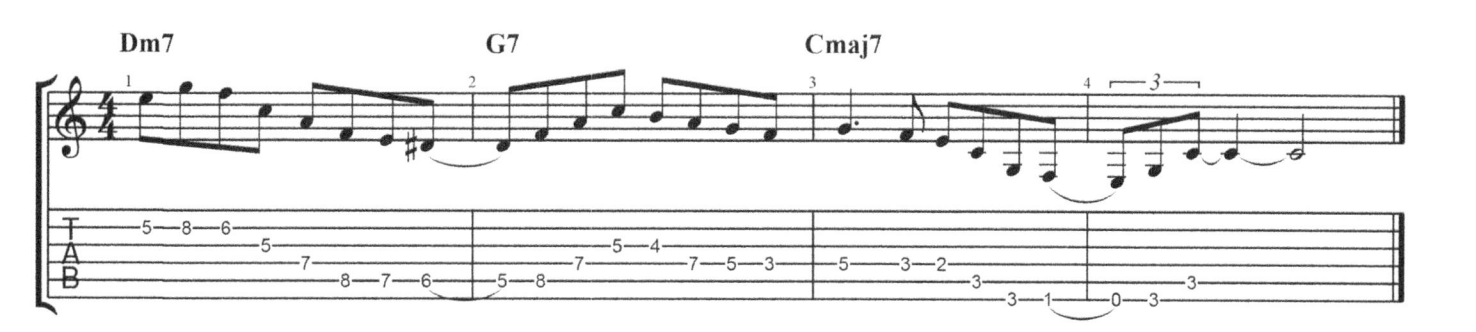

The next two ideas are both modern sounding string skipping lines. The first of these is played as continuous 1/8th notes with the wide intervals adding interest. To make the line really swing, try picking the notes that fall on the "**&**" beats (1**&**, 2**&** etc) a little harder than the rest. Listen to the audio to catch my phrasing.

Example 1z

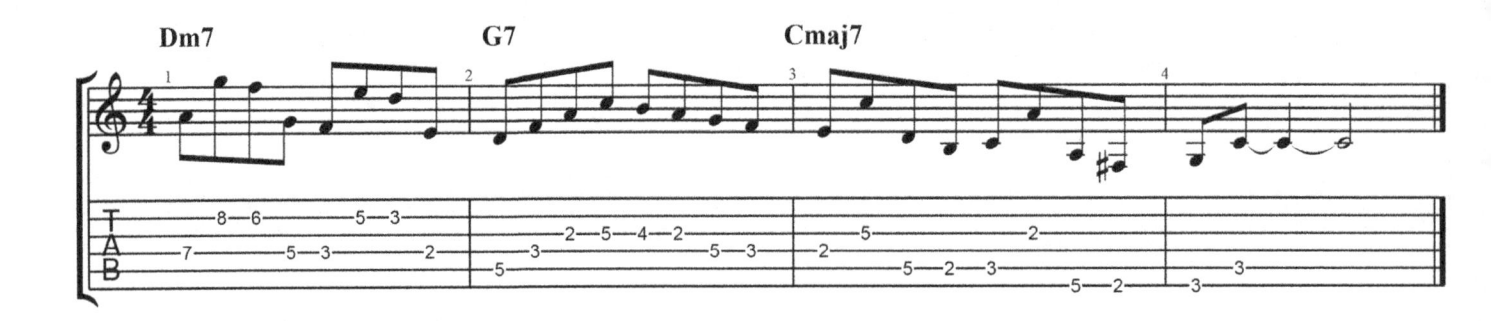

The second string skipping ideas uses triplets and the phrasing idea is repeated across bars.

Example 1z1

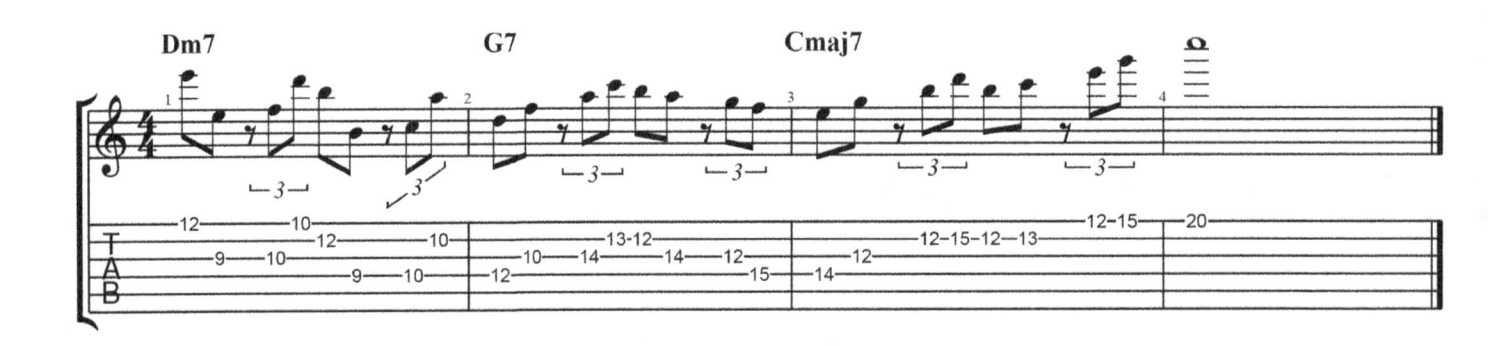

Finally, here are five lines that use Cell 4 – the Mixolydian from the b7 of G7.

First, here's a staple bebop line that uses swung 1/8th notes to spell out the Dm7 to G7 bars before breaking up the rhythm in bar three.

Example 1z2

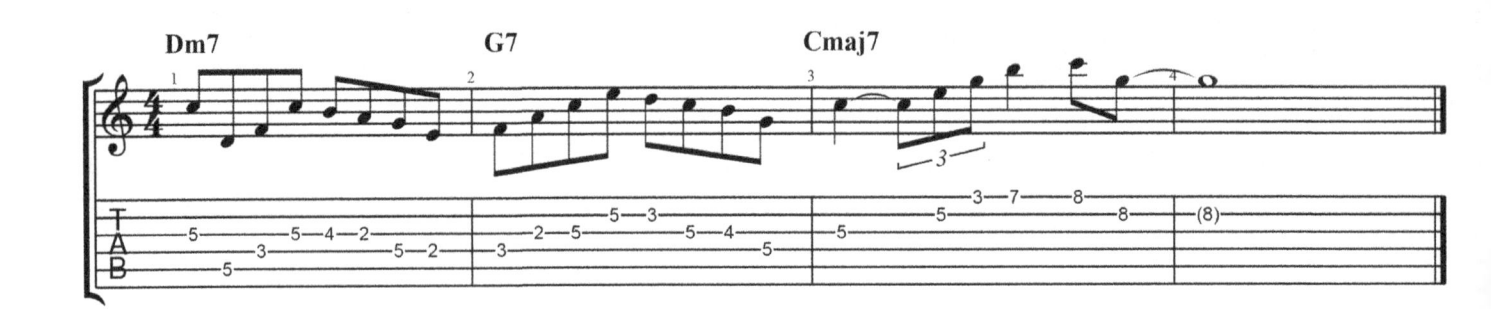

Here's another line that uses side stepping movements in bar one to create a tension that is resolved by the cell in bar two. You can probably visualize in bar one that I've played two scale notes, then experimented with descending in half steps. Again, the cell is used to remind us of the core harmony and provide a smooth transition to the I chord.

Example 1z3

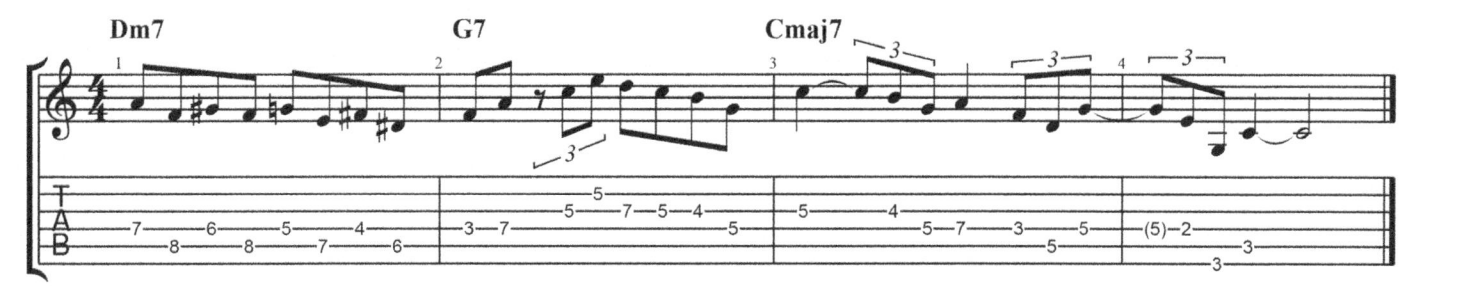

Next up is another must-know bebop lick, which uses the range of the neck to end on a high C root note in bar four.

Example 1z4

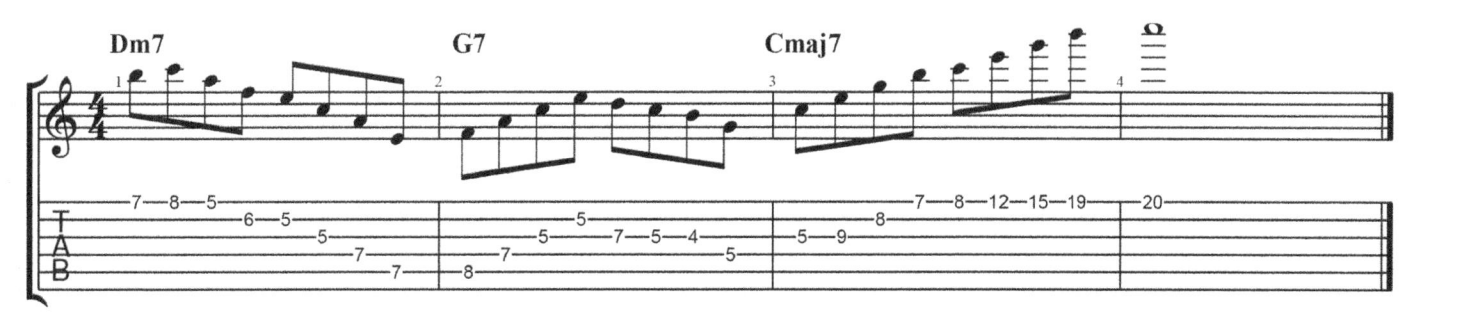

This Cell 4 line uses some strategically placed passing notes to spice up the line, which ends with a bluesy lick.

Example 1z5

To end this chapter, here's one more 1/8th note idea that uses string skips in bar one to add movement to the phrase. The phrasing in bar one can be tricky to execute at the tempo of the audio example, so make sure you're picking it cleanly.

Example 1z6

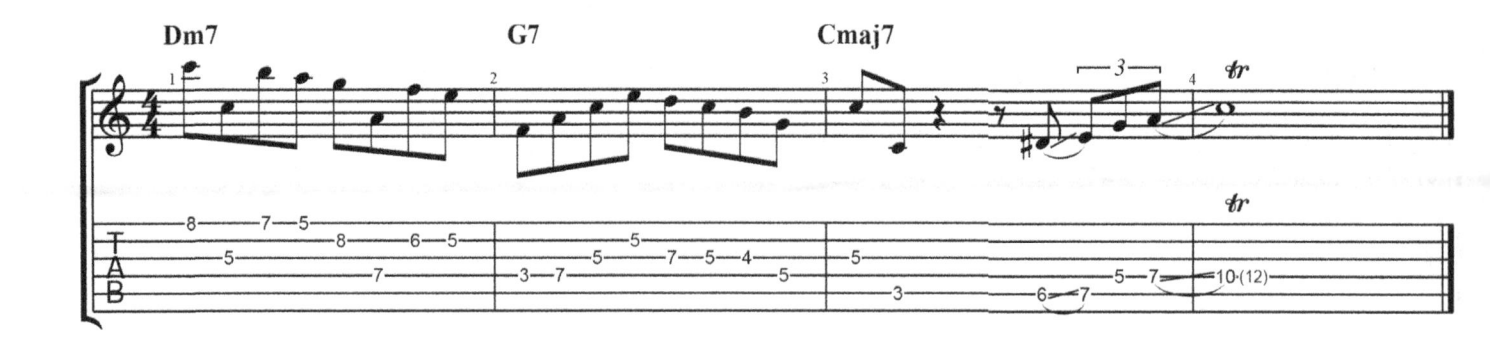

Chapter Two – Whole Tone Scale Cells

We've looked at the concept of melodic cells using the Mixolydian scale and learned lots of different approaches to building lines with the cell at the heart of them. However, we can use other scales to create our dominant chord cells. The dominant 7 chord lends itself to being altered, so for the rest of this book we'll turn our attention to the use of altered scales to create more exotic melodic cells, beginning with the Whole Tone scale.

The Whole Tone scale is a scale built entirely from whole step intervals. It is a *hexatonic* scale, meaning that there are only six tones per octave. Its perfectly symmetrical shape means that it has an ambiguous, unresolved sound, which makes it very useful for adding altered colors to our solos. Its "outside" sound also makes it more obvious when we're arrived back "home" to the I chord.

A triad built on any note of the Whole Tone scale is always augmented, and the entire scale can be expressed by playing two augmented triads a major second apart. This makes it especially useful for playing over dominant chords, as we'll see below.

The G Whole Tone scale

To understand how the Whole Tone scale functions over a dominant chord, it's useful to compare it to the G Mixolydian scale from the previous chapter. Here's a reminder of the notes/intervals of G Mixolydian:

G	A	B	C	D	E	F
Root	2nd	3rd	4th	5th	6th	b7

Now, here are the notes of G Whole Tone and the intervals it highlights when played over a 7 chord.

G	A	B	C#	D#	F
Root	9th	3rd	b5	#5	b7

The G Whole Tone scale brings out the b5 and #5 tensions over G7, as well as adding an extended A note, which creates a G9 sound.

Scale shapes

Below are the sixth and fifth string root shapes for this scale. I've shown the two main positions I like to use for it.

Because of its symmetrical shape, with equally spaced intervals, there are a few different approaches to playing this scale, but I have found the following shapes to be both economical and easy to navigate. First, the sixth string root shape.

G Whole Tone

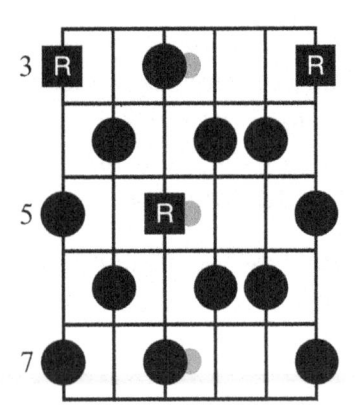

Notice that for the fifth string root shape, I've added the scale notes on the sixth string too (indicated by hollow notes) to complete the pattern. Doing this means that both shapes now have a 3 2 3 2 2 3 note-per-string pattern.

G Whole Tone

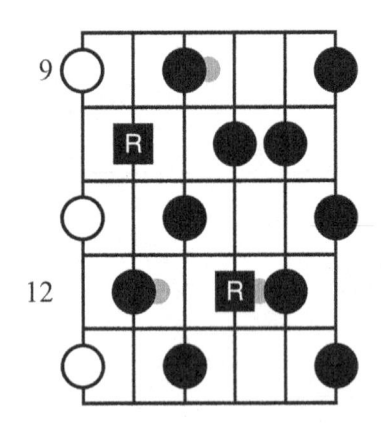

The melodic cells

Using the exact same method as the previous chapter, we'll now take the chord tones of G7 (G B D F) and use the G Whole Tone scale to build 4 melodic cells – one from each chord tone. Each melodic line will outline the G7 chord, then resolve to the I chord (Cmaj7).

First, from the G root note. Listening to this line, you can immediately hear the effect of using an altered scale to form the cell. It's like a formula for "instant bebop" because the altered tensions pop out, and the resolution from the Whole Tone to the root of the Cmaj7 chord sounds like an enclosure lick at the end.

Example 2a – Cell 1

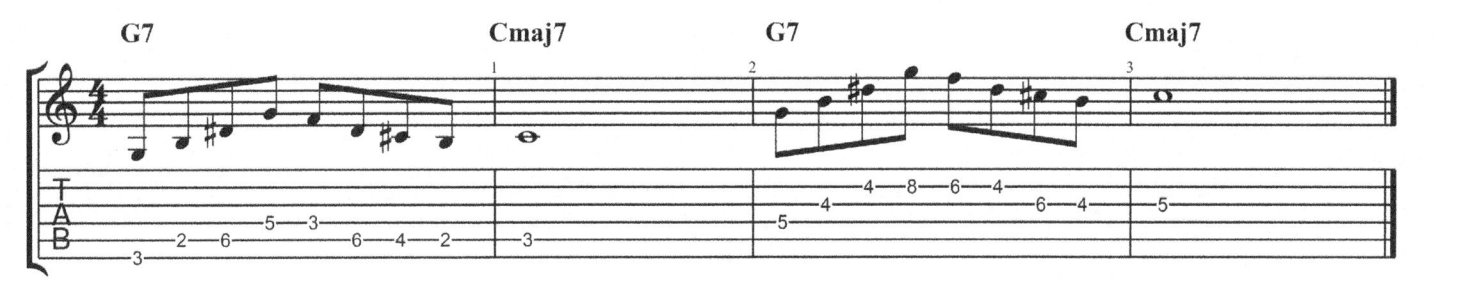

Next, we'll play the cell from the 3rd (B). This line resolves to the 3rd of the Cmaj7 chord, as it's a nice half step movement from Whole Tone to chord tone.

Example 2b – Cell 2

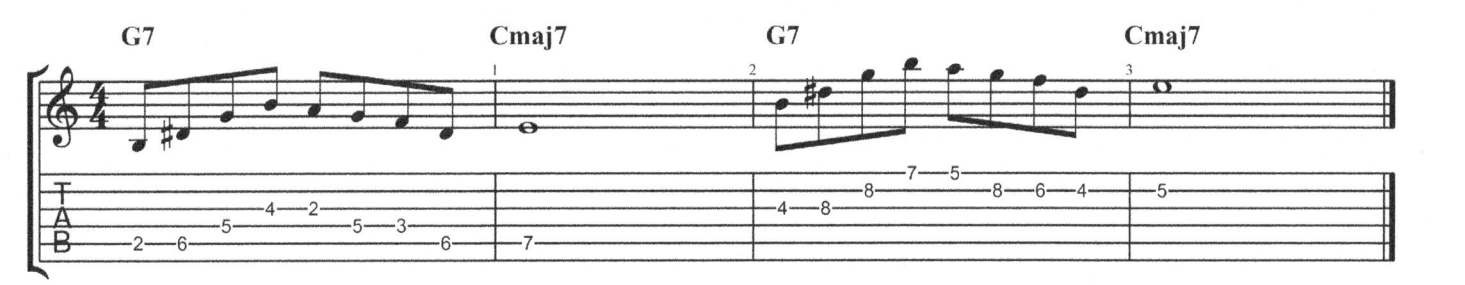

Here's where things get interesting. The 5th of the G7 chord is a D note, but the G Whole Tone scale contains a D# rather than a D. So, when we build the melodic scale from the 5th, we do so from the #5 (D#) instead. Beginning with an altered note on a downbeat gives this cell a tense outside sound from the get-go.

Example 2c – Cell 3

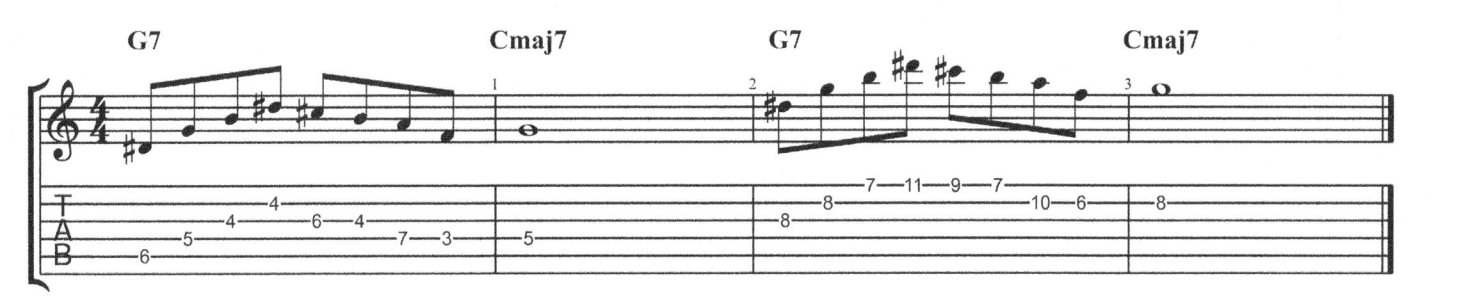

And finally, Cell 4, from the b7 (F).

Example 2d – Cell 4

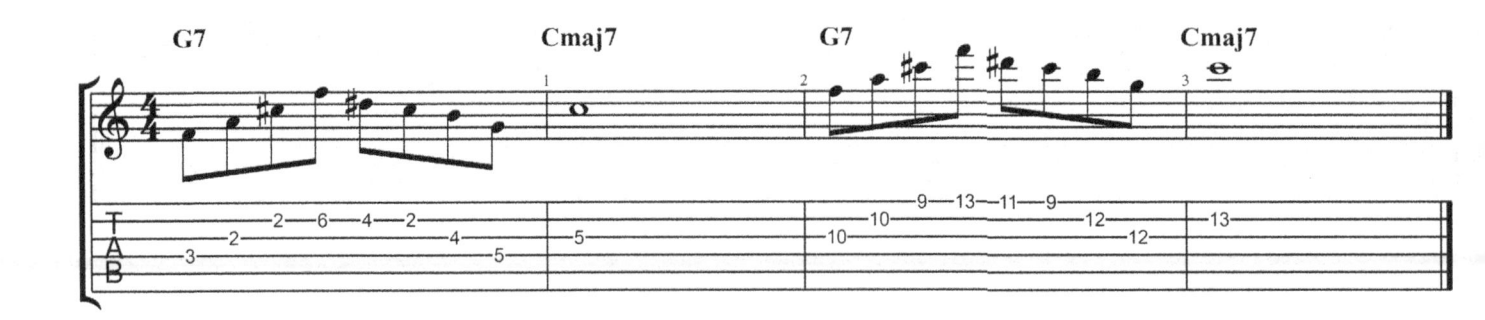

Putting the cells into a Major ii V I

Now that we've created four melodic cells using the Whole Tone scale, let's hear how they sound in the context of the Major ii V I progression. We'll begin by playing two simple lines for each cell.

Example 2e

Here's the first line that uses Cell 1, from the G root note.

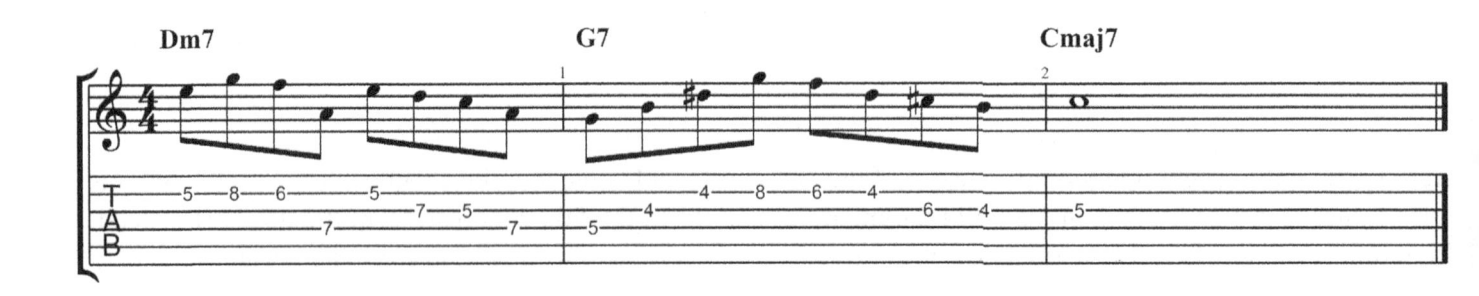

And another simple Cell 1 line with more rhythmic variation in bar one.

Example 2f

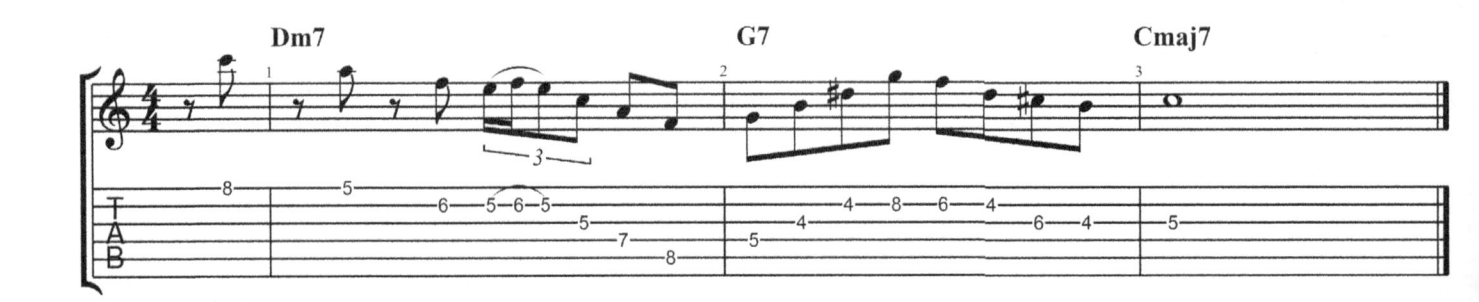

Next, Cell 2 from 3rd (B). Notice how beginning on the 3rd allows this cell to add some real color to the line.

Example 2g

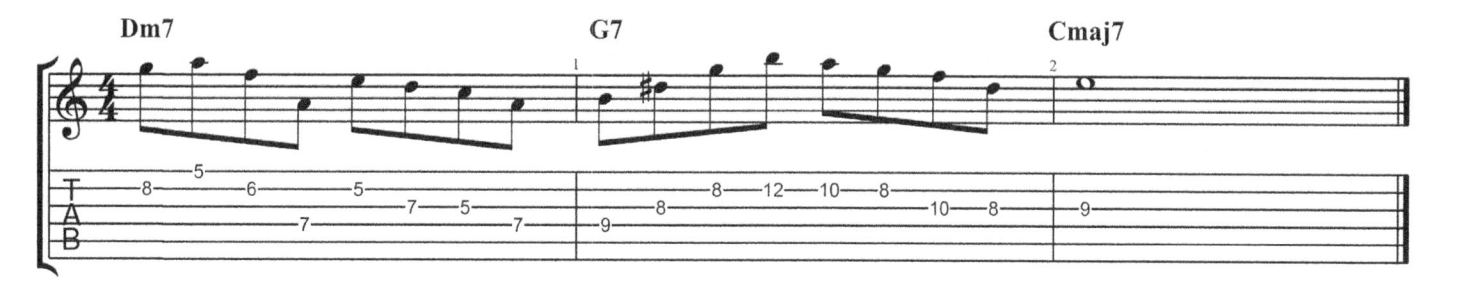

Here's the second Cell 2 line.

Example 2h

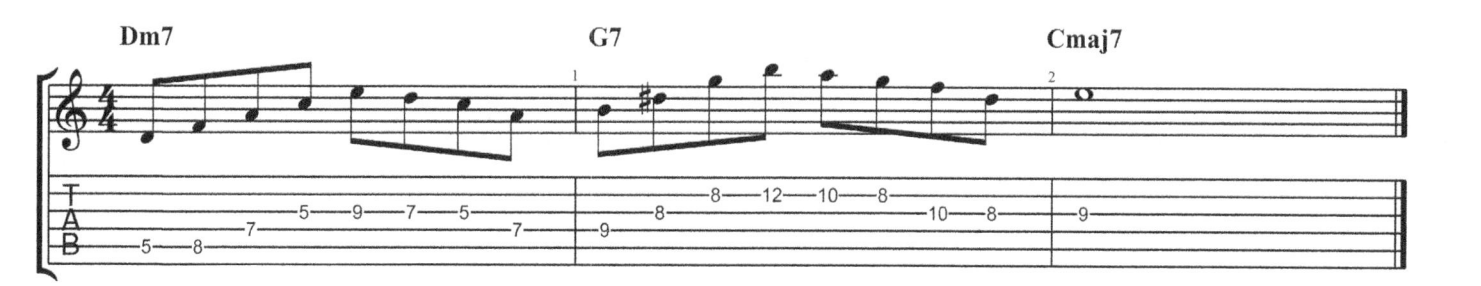

Next is a line using Cell 3, launching from the #5 (D#). You may have noticed that the first three notes of Cell 3 form a G augmented triad inversion (D# G B). This is characteristic of the Whole Tone sound and these augmented shapes can be moved around the fretboard in major 3rds (a distance of four frets) when improvising.

Example 2i

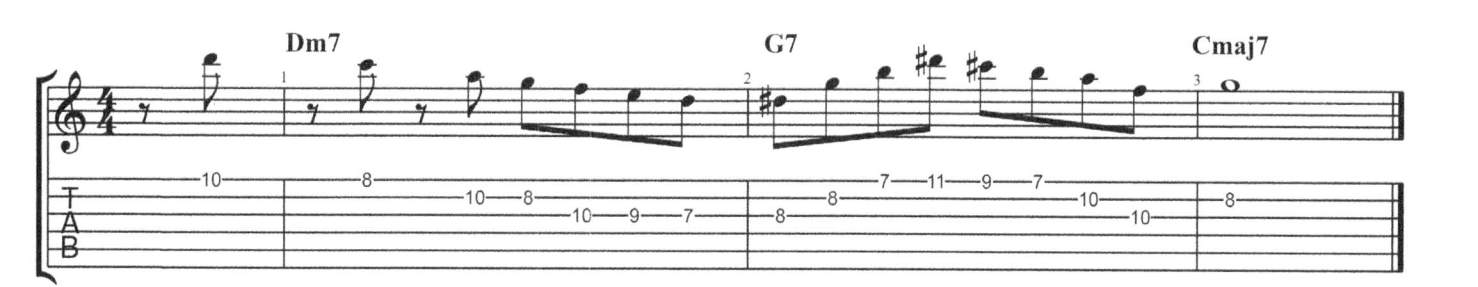

Here is the second Cell 3 line.

Example 2j

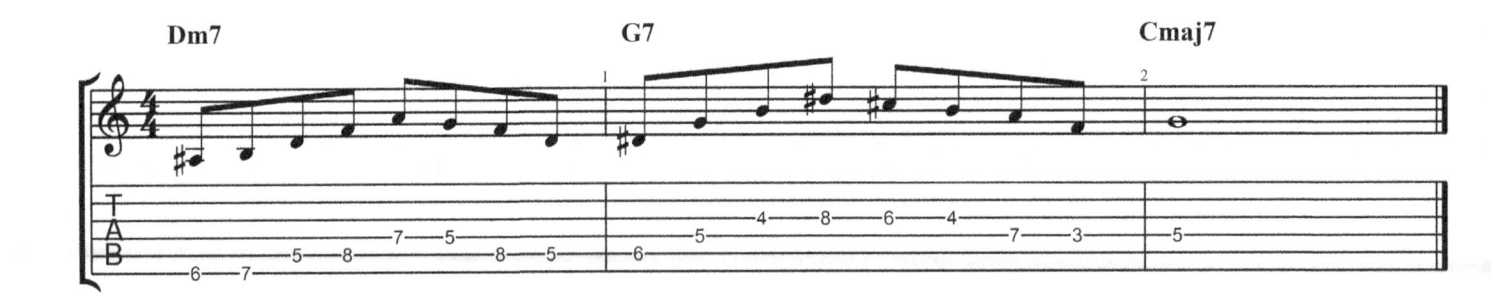

Cell 4, from the b7 (F) resolves tidily to the root of Cmaj7 with a perfect 4th interval.

Example 2k

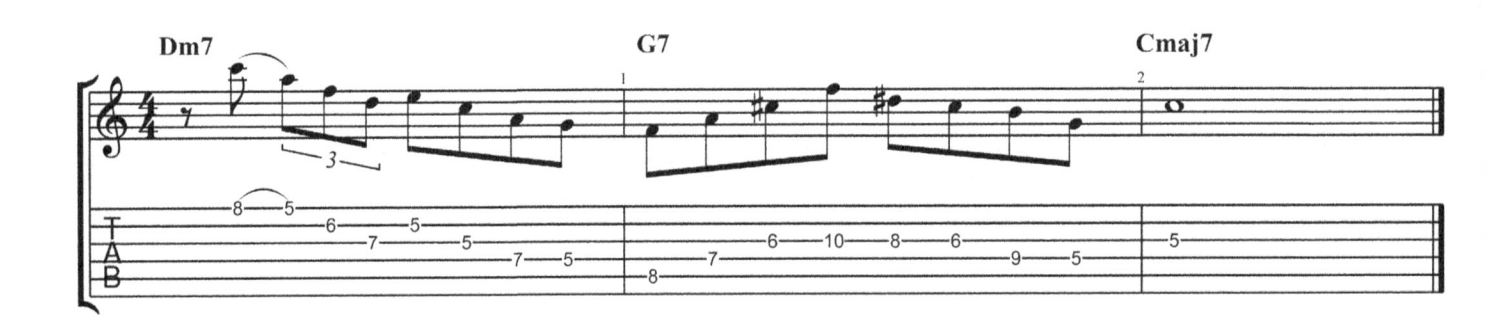

Here's an alternative approach using Cell 4.

Example 2l

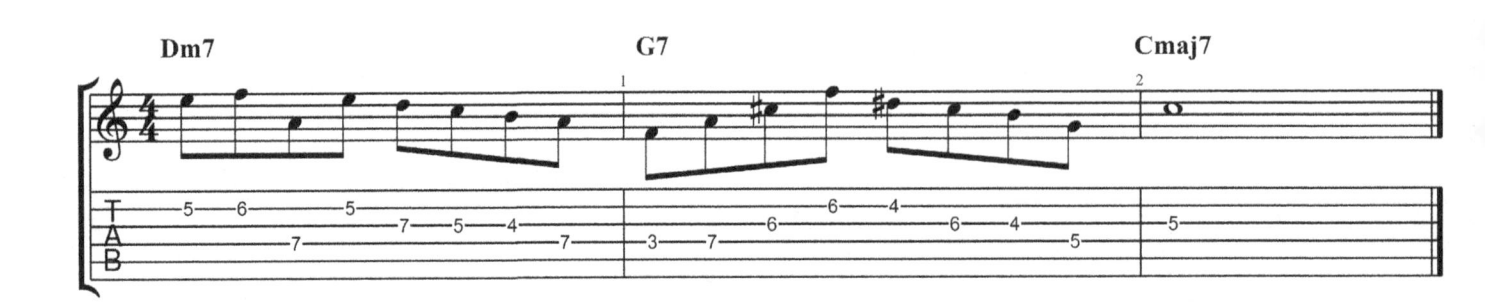

More advanced cellular vocabulary

Now that we have embedded the sound of the Whole Tone cells in our ears and become more familiar with their cadence, we can get more creative and introduce rhythmic variation to alter the phrasing. We'll use all of the rhythmic devices covered in Chapter One to break things up and play more interesting, less predictable lines.

We're going to learn five lines for each of the four cells. First, five ideas that use Cell 1, and we kick off with a bebop style line that has a rhythmic consistency across the three main bars.

Example 2m

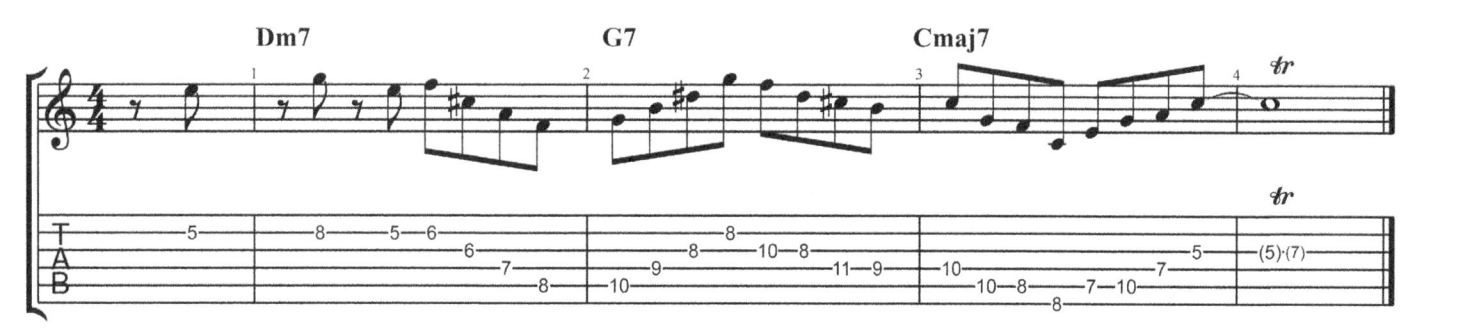

For the second line, we're going to play the notes of G Whole Tone over the Dm7 chord, treating the ii and V chords as the same basic "sound", as well as playing Cell 1 over the G7 chord. The resolution to the I chord is achieved with a bluesy lick. Check out the audio and hear the more contemporary sound that can be achieved by playing the altered scale over the ii as well as the V chord.

Example 2n

In bar one of Example 2o, we're using the D Melodic Minor scale (D E F G A B C#) over the Dm7 chord. It hints at the Whole Tone sound, as they share the characteristic b5 (C#) interval. Beginning on the b5 adds some surprise to this lick.

Example 2o

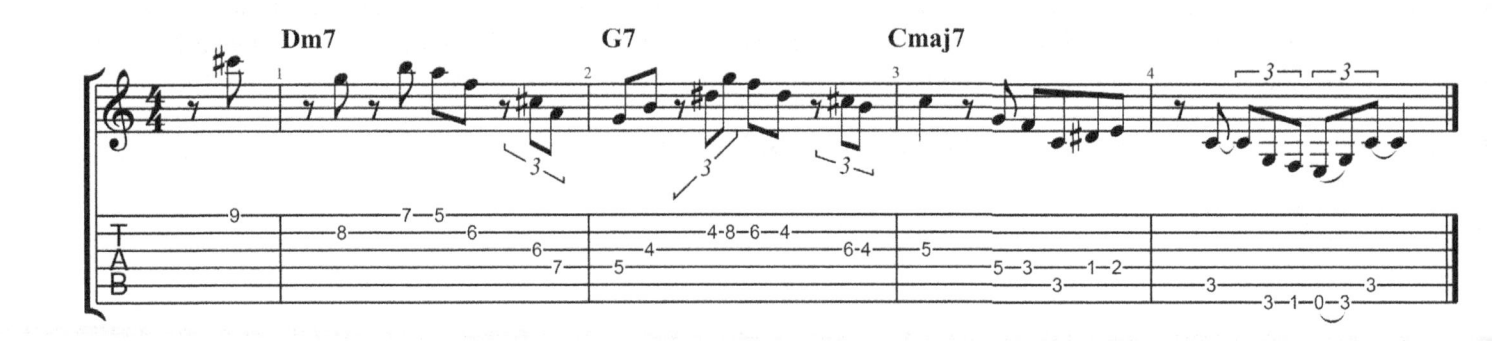

Example 2p continues with the idea of using G Whole Tone over the Dm7 chord, and this lick begins with 3rd intervals before moving into the cell.

Example 2p

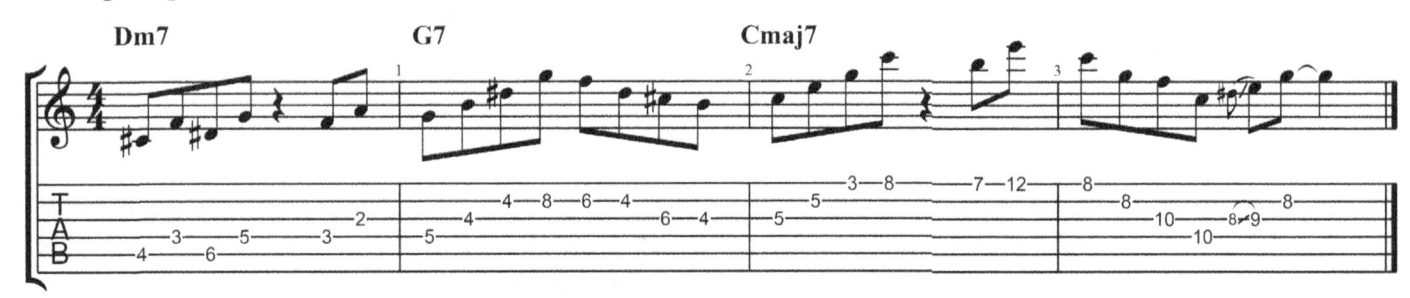

Here, bars 1-2 use G Whole Tone to create a question and answer style phrase.

Example 2q

Next we have five example lines that use Cell 2, launching from the 3rd (B). This line begins on the outside sounding C# of the G Whole Tone scale.

Example 2r

In this example the cell is broken up with a triplet in the middle and mirrors the phrasing of bar one.

Example 2s

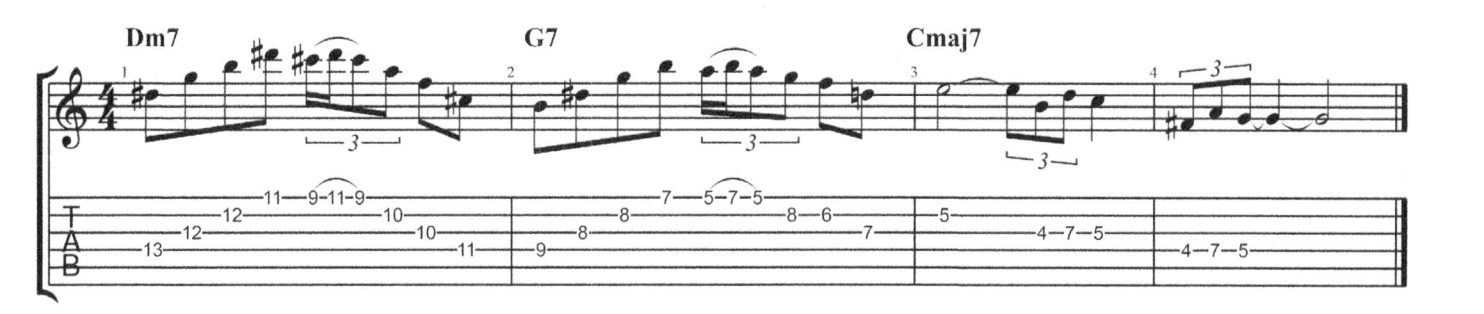

Here's a more angular phrase to open the next line

Example 2t

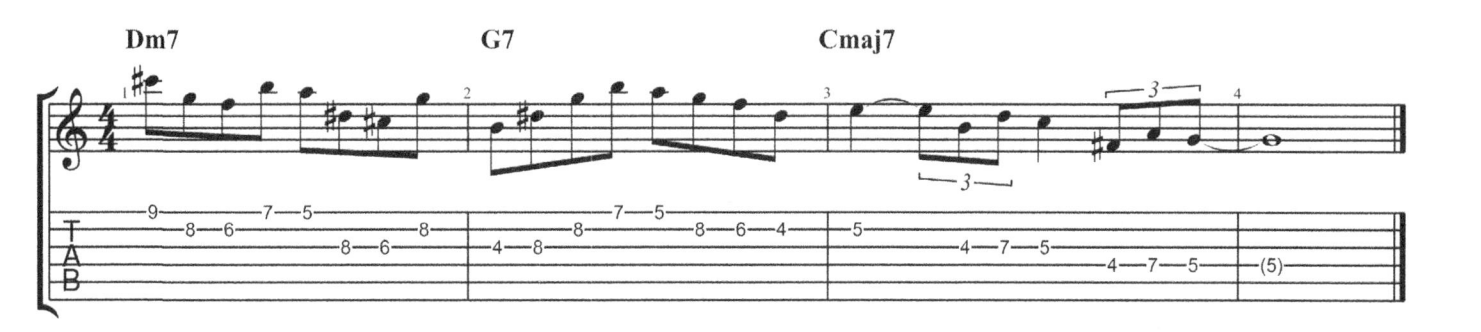

The next lick begins with some unusual 2nd interval phrasing, with the lower notes in bar one displaced by an octave. This idea really emphasizes the character of the Whole Tone.

Example 2u

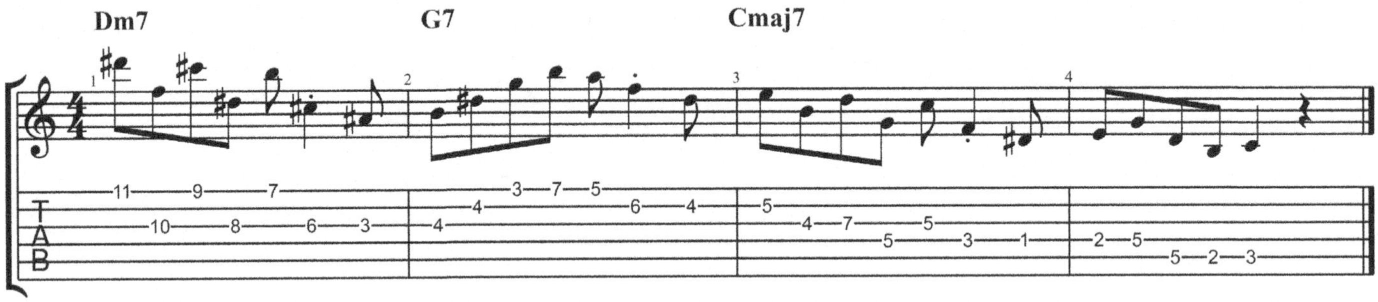
Dm7
G7
Cmaj7

Here's one more example that uses Cell 2.

Example 2v

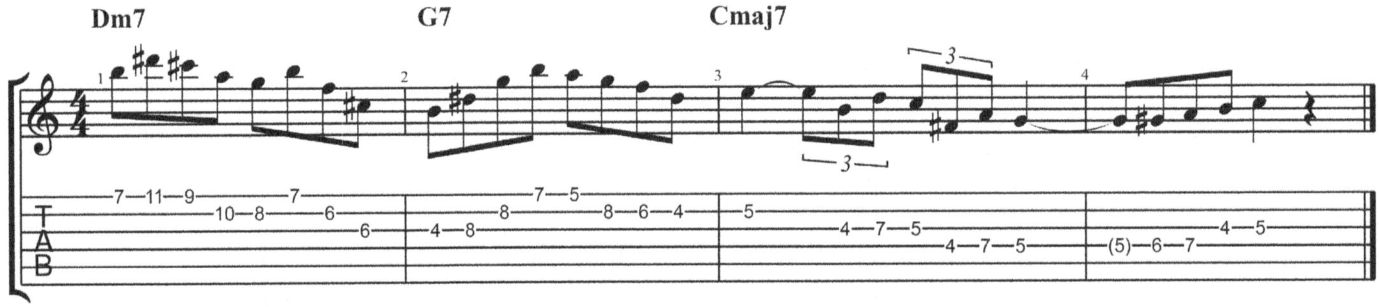
Dm7
G7
Cmaj7

Now onto some examples that use Cell 3, built from the #5 (D#) of G7.

In this set of examples, notice that each time the cell resolves to a G note over Cmaj7. It's more common to resolve to the root or 3rd, but I like this whole step resolution that is in keeping with the character of the Whole Tone scale.

Example 2w

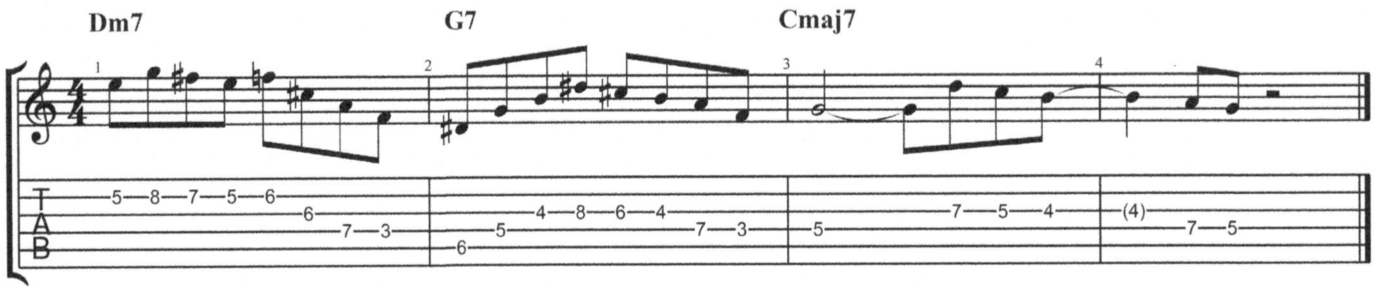
Dm7
G7
Cmaj7

The next line calls for a string skip at the beginning of bar two. Work out your fingering before playing this lick up to tempo to get the transition sounding seamless.

Example 2x

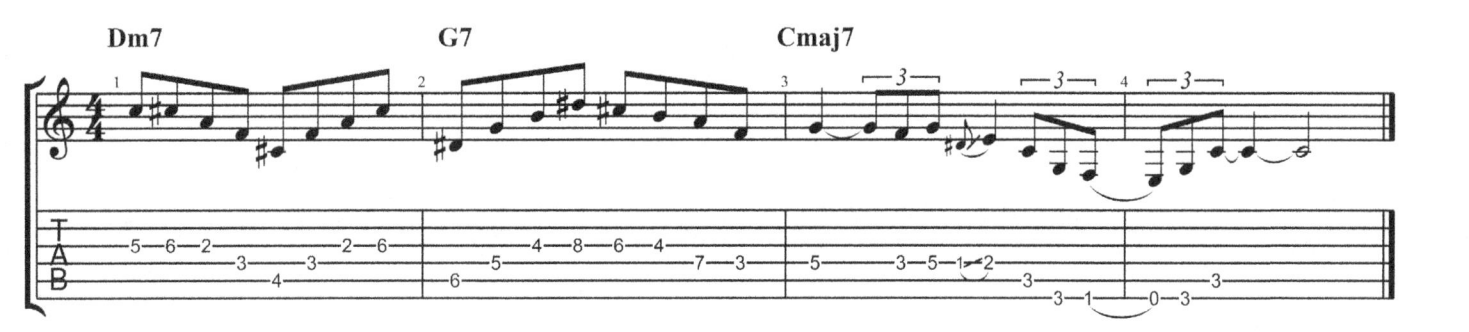

The broken phrasing of the next example, with regular 1/8th note rests, helps it to cut against the swing feel of the backing.

Example 2y

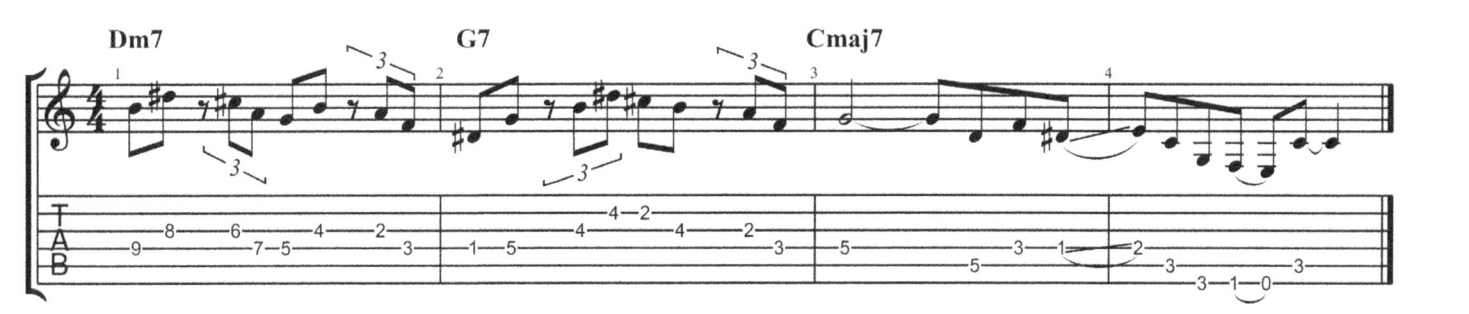

Our fourth Cell 3 example uses very wide intervals to achieve a more modern sound. It's easy to fall into the trap of playing stepwise patterns in jazz, especially when the chord changes are moving quickly. Playing with a more intervallic approach will immediately set you apart as a player, so do work on this idea during your practice sessions.

Example 2z

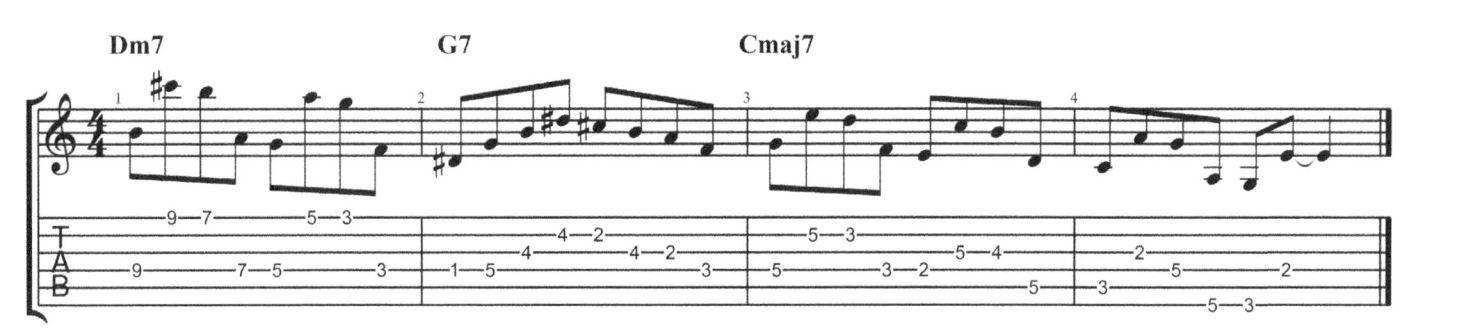

In this final Cell 3 example, look out for the slurred 1/16th note triplets in bars 3-4 over Cmaj7. Listen to the audio to capture my phrasing.

Example 2z1

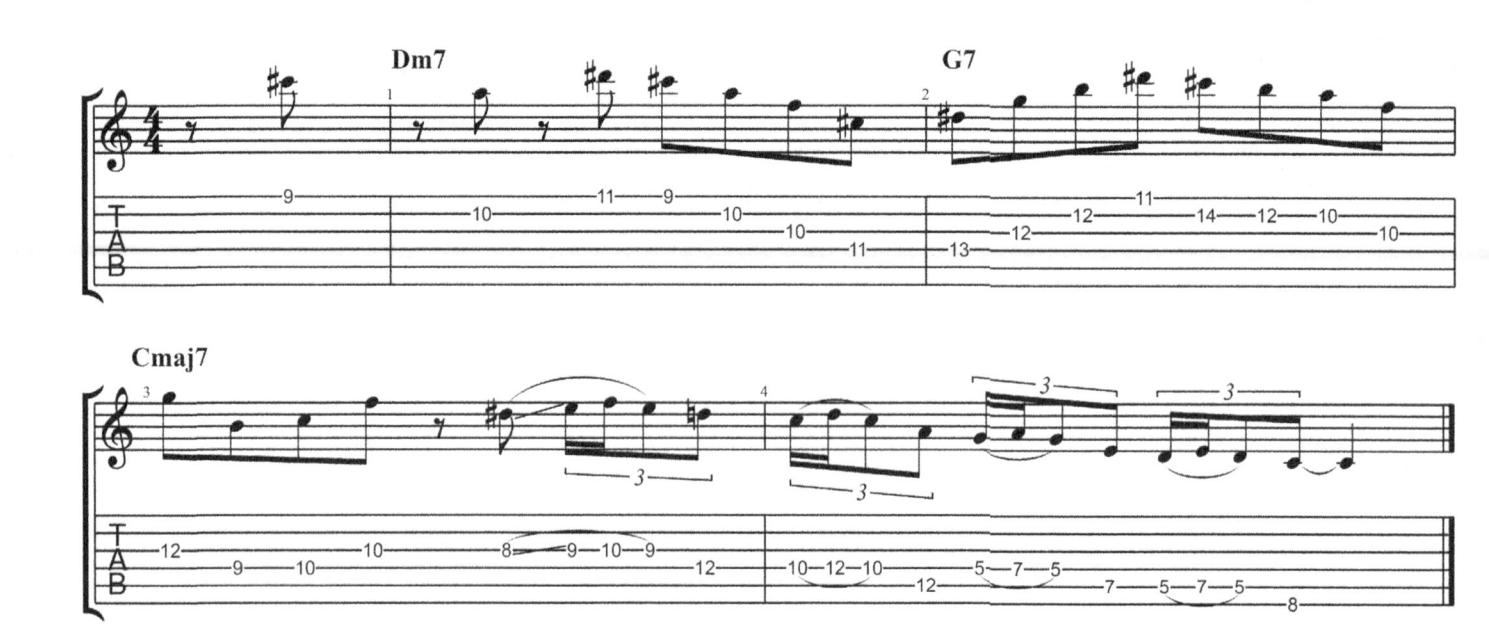

Now, here is a collection of lines that use Cell 4, built from the b7 (F) chord tone of G7. With these lines, it often makes sense to resolve to the root of Cmaj7 via a 4th interval, though this is not a hard and fast rule.

Bar one of Example 2z2 uses the D Melodic Minor scale again. The F# note that lands on beat 4 doesn't belong to the scale but is a passing note that is targeting the F note on beat 1 of bar two.

Example 2z2

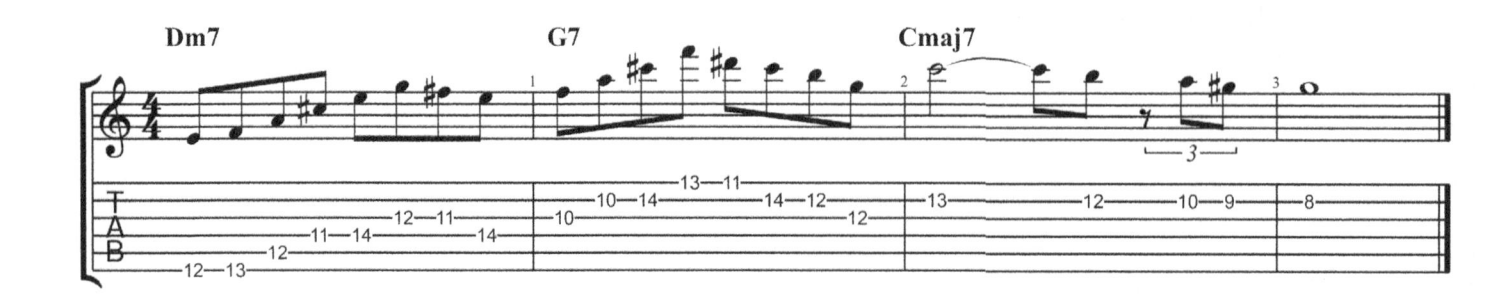

This line uses the Whole Tone in bar one and sequences it with alternating 4ths and 3rd intervals.

Example 2z3

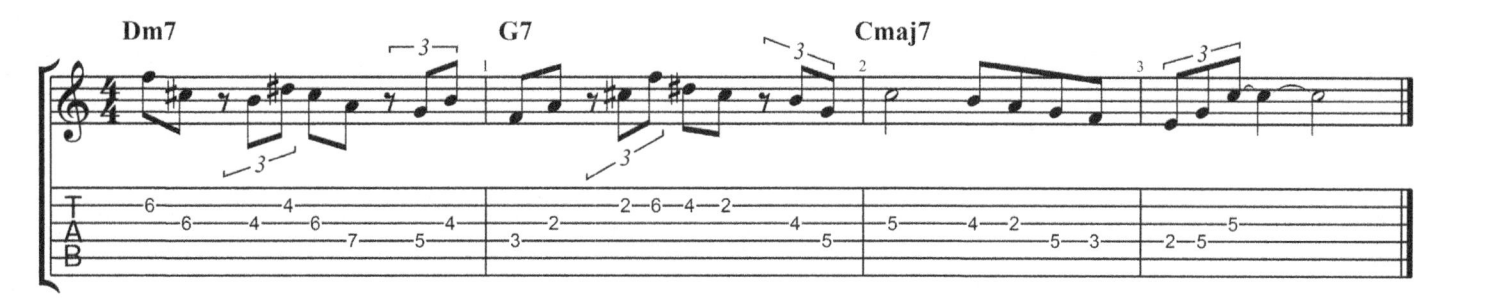

Next up, a line that ebbs and flows, nicely disguising the cell in bar two.

Example 2z4

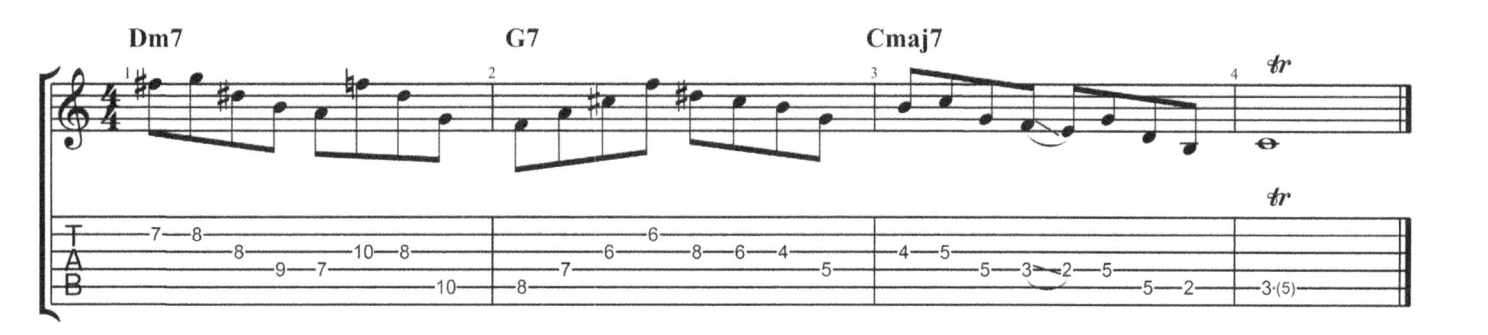

Look out for the 1/8th note triplet rest in the middle of the cell in bar two of the next line – it's designed to break up the predictable phrasing.

Example 2z5

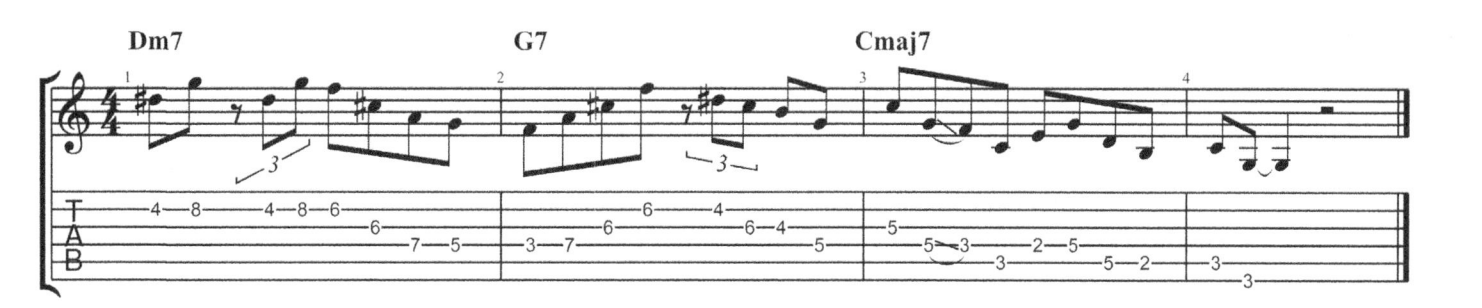

This last line mimics the phrasing of the cell in bar one. This phrase uses G Whole Tone but mainly emphasizes the D# altered note.

Example 2z6

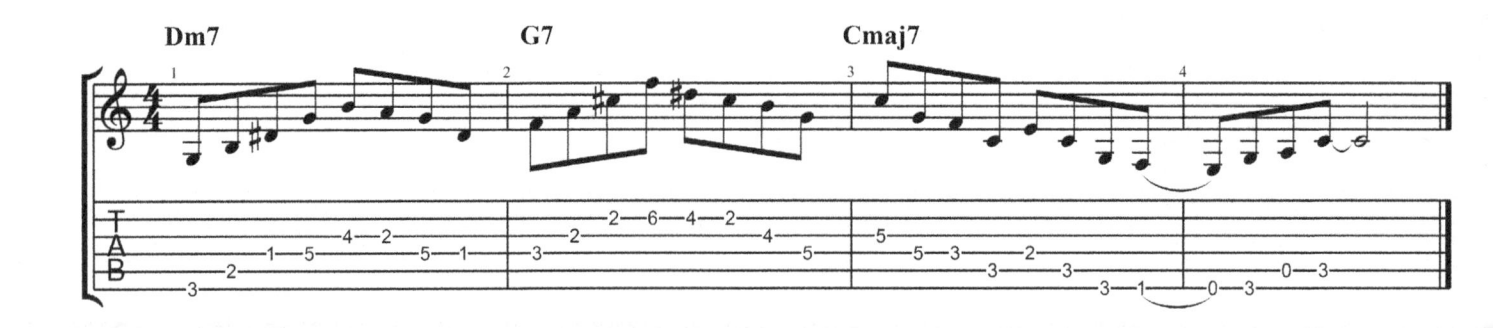

Whole Tone Melodic Cells in a Minor ii V i

So far, we've played all of our melodic ideas over the Major ii V I chord sequence, but altered scales also shine in a minor ii V i setting – a sequence that is just as important as its major counterpart in learning jazz. So now, we are going to repeat our process, but this time oriented toward the minor ii V i.

As before, we'll begin by establishing the dominant chord cells that will be the core of each line. These will be similar to the major cells from earlier, but now we're required to resolve to a slightly different set of chord tones.

This time, our ii V i sequence is Dm7b5 – G7 – Cm7 and the examples in this chapter will be notated in the key of C Minor.

Here is Minor Cell 1, built from the G root note.

Example 2z7 – Minor Cell 1

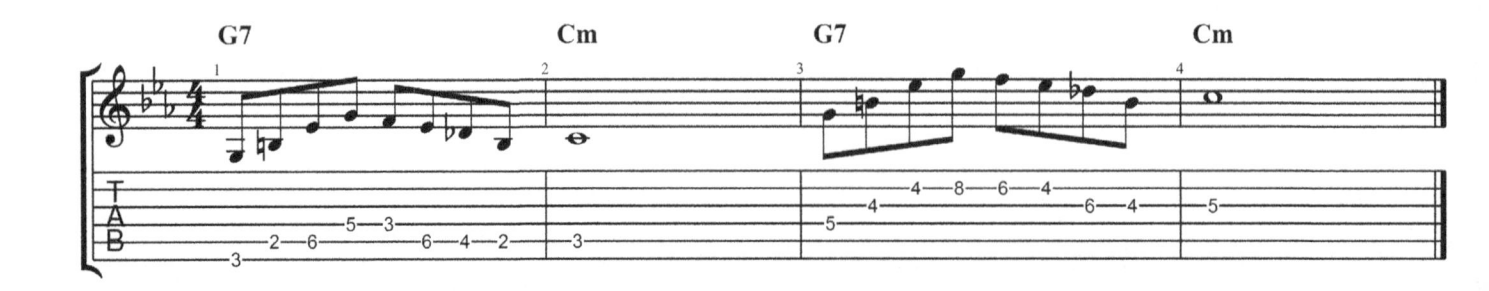

Next, Minor Cell 2 from 3rd (B).

Example 2z8 – Minor Cell 2

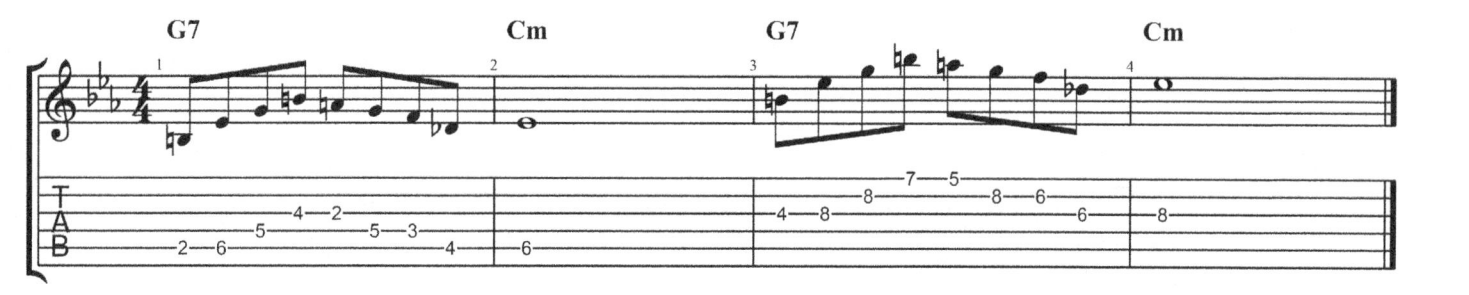

When it comes to Minor Cell 3, remember that we can't begin the cell on a D note (the 5th of G7), because there is no D note in the G Whole Tone scale. Instead, we launch it from the #5 interval.

Example 2z9 – Minor Cell 3

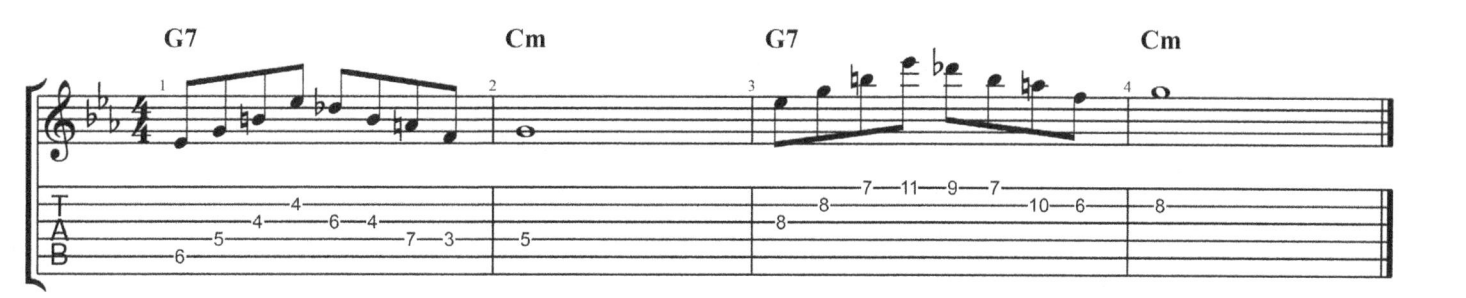

Lastly, Minor Cell 4 is built from the b7 (F).

Example 2z10 – Minor Cell 4

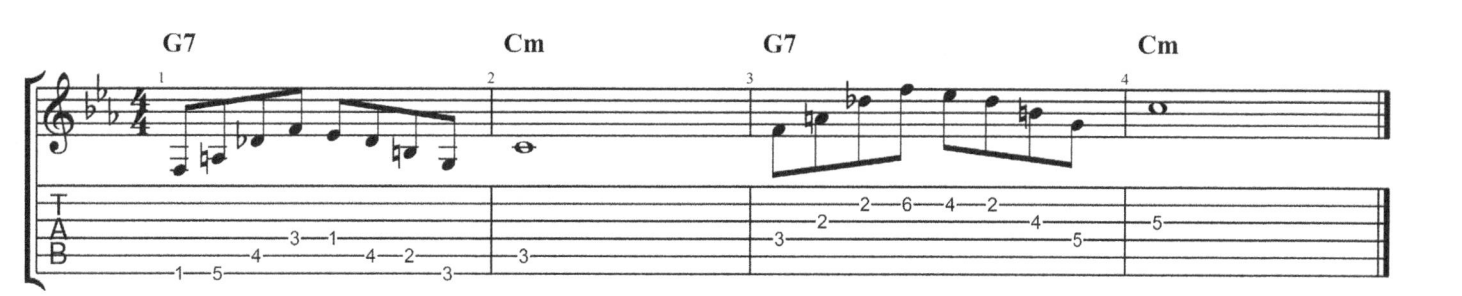

Putting the cells into a Minor ii V I

Now we'll play these four cells in the context of the minor ii V i. There are two simple examples for each cell. I won't explain each line, as you get the idea by now, but play through them a few times and listen to the effect of the cell in a minor ii V i sequence. Aim to commit each cell to memory.

First, two Cell 1 minor ii V i lines.

Example 2z11

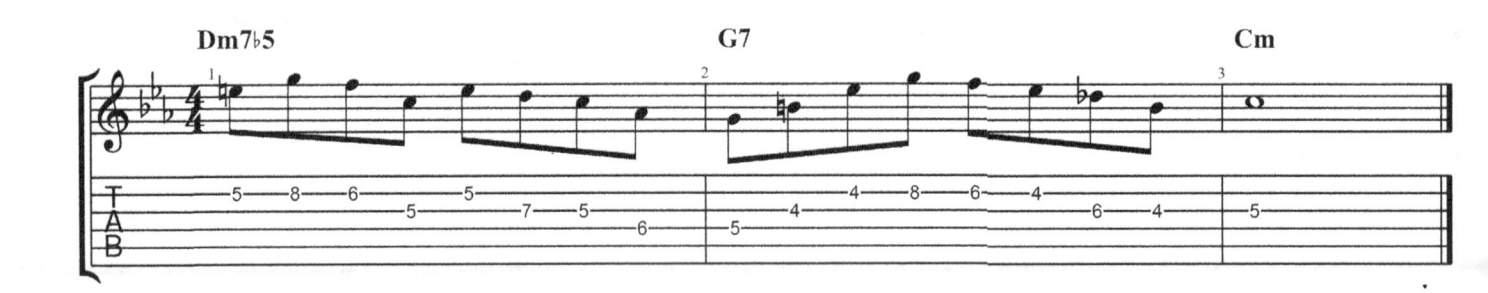

Example 2z12

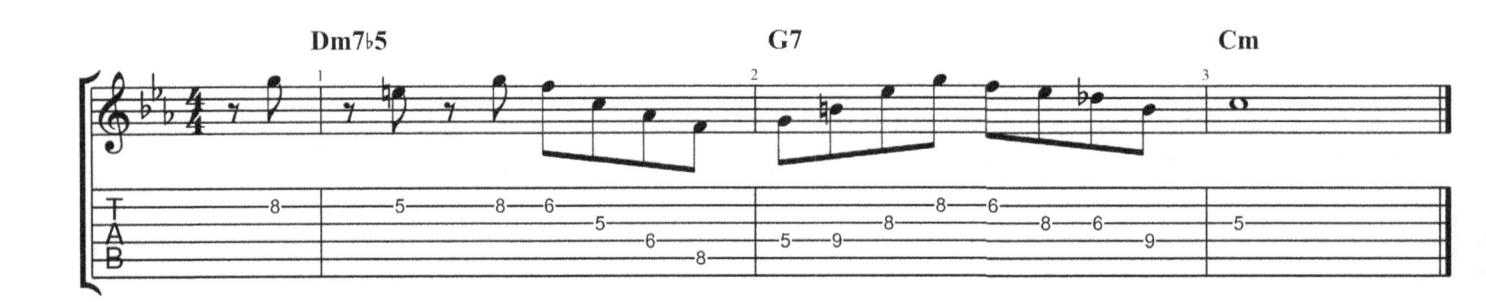

Next, two basic Cell 2 minor ii V i ideas.

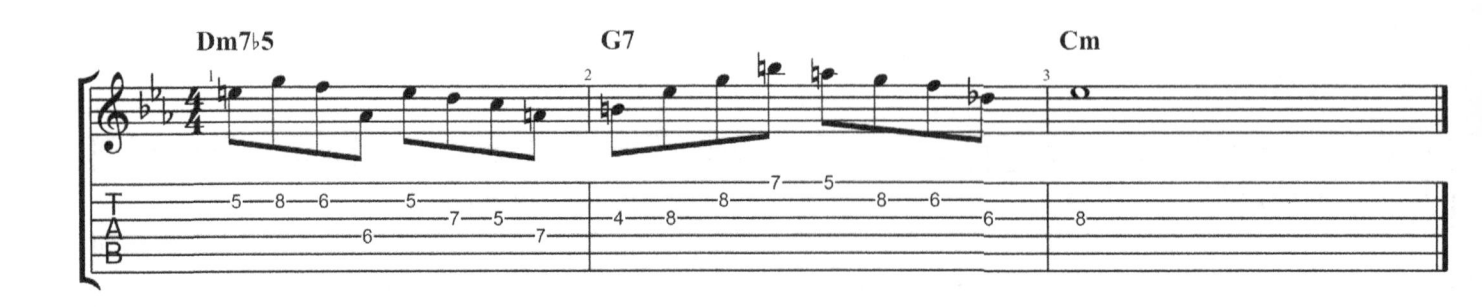

Example 2z13

Example 2z14

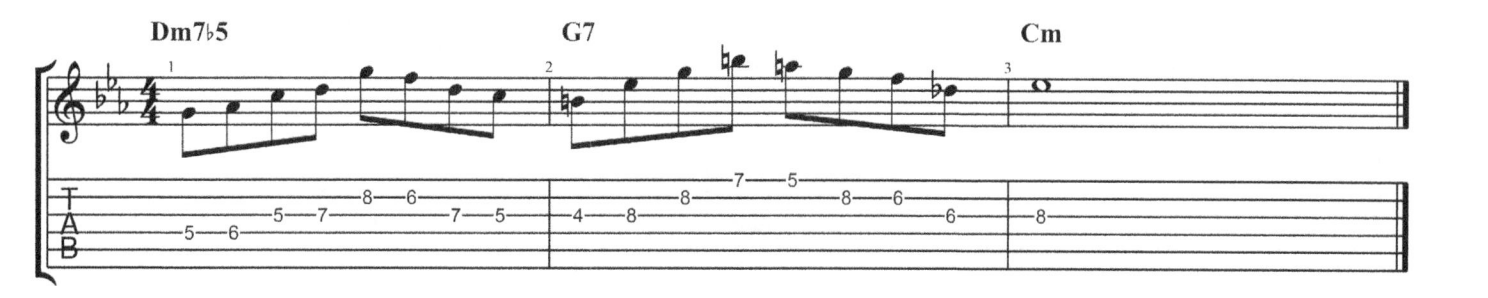

Here are two examples using Cell 3.

Example 2z15

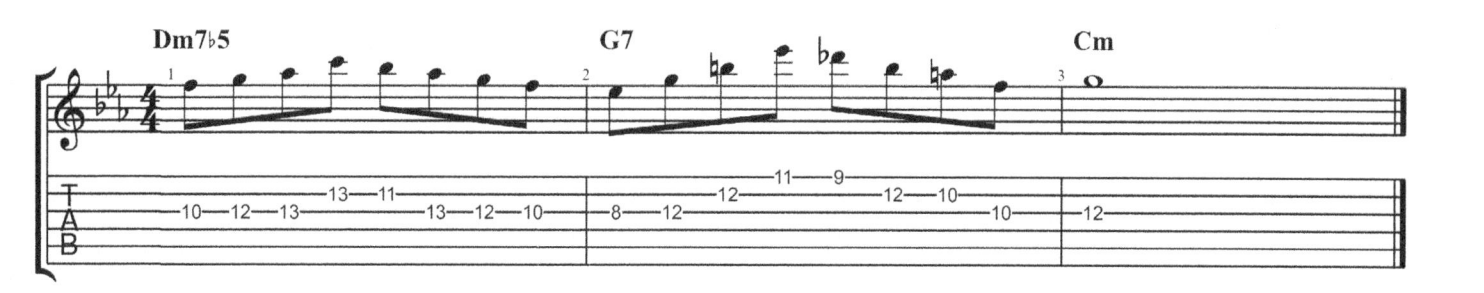

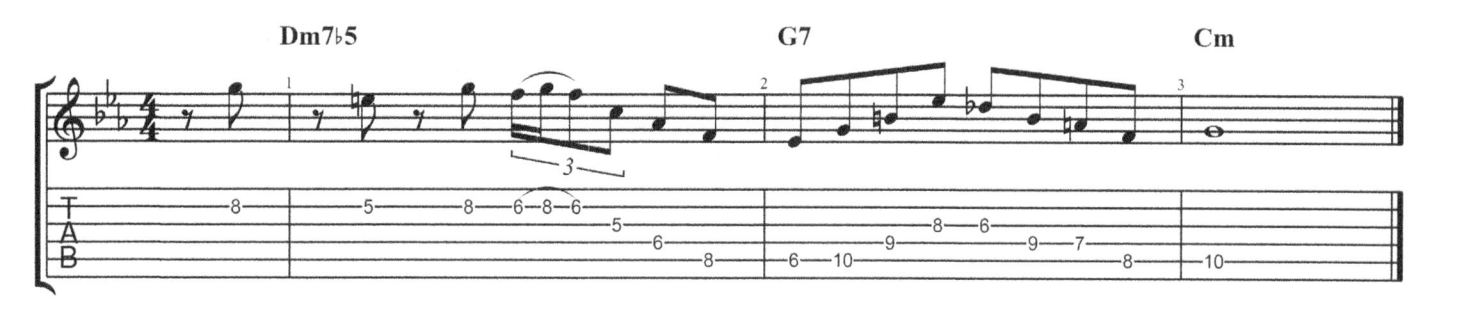

Example 2z16

And two simple lines for Cell 4.

Example 2z17

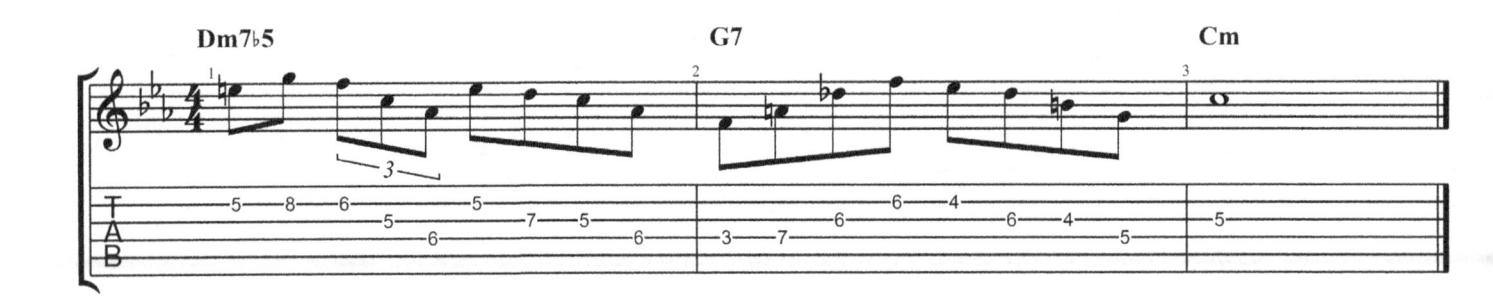

Example 2z18

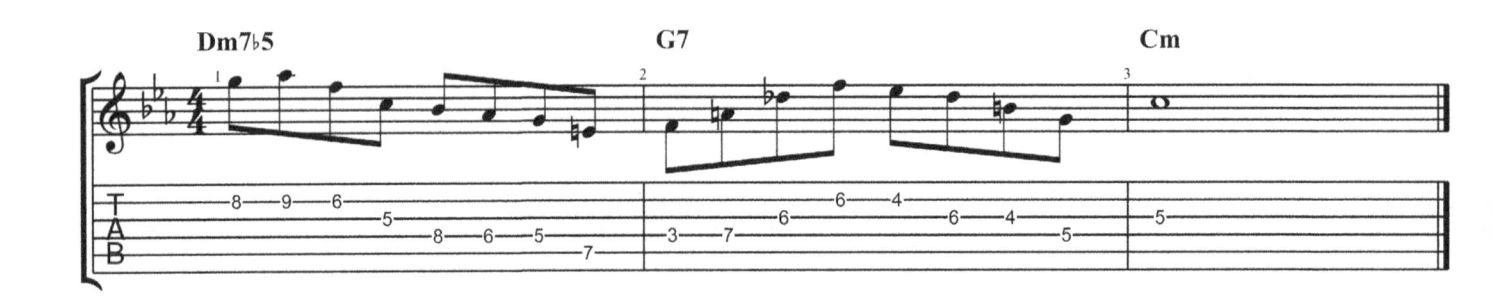

More advanced cellular vocabulary

Next, we're going add rhythmic variation to turn these cellular ideas into instantly useable licks. Remember, whenever you encounter a line that you particularly like, be sure to transpose it into other keys and test it out over a favorite jazz standard. First, here are five lines that use Cell 1, from the root of G7.

Our first line uses a fast triplet phrase in bar one. Listen to the audio to get the articulation right. The triplet figures here and in bar three help to keep this line swinging.

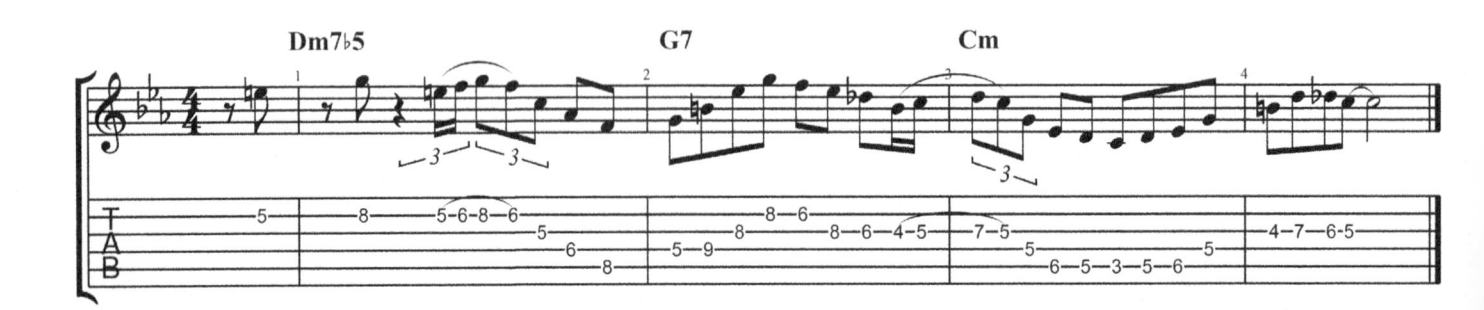

Example 2z19

In the next example, the shape of the phrase in bars one and three is identical, which helps to glue the whole line together. In bar three, the notes are from the C Melodic Minor scale (C D Eb F G A B).

Example 2z20

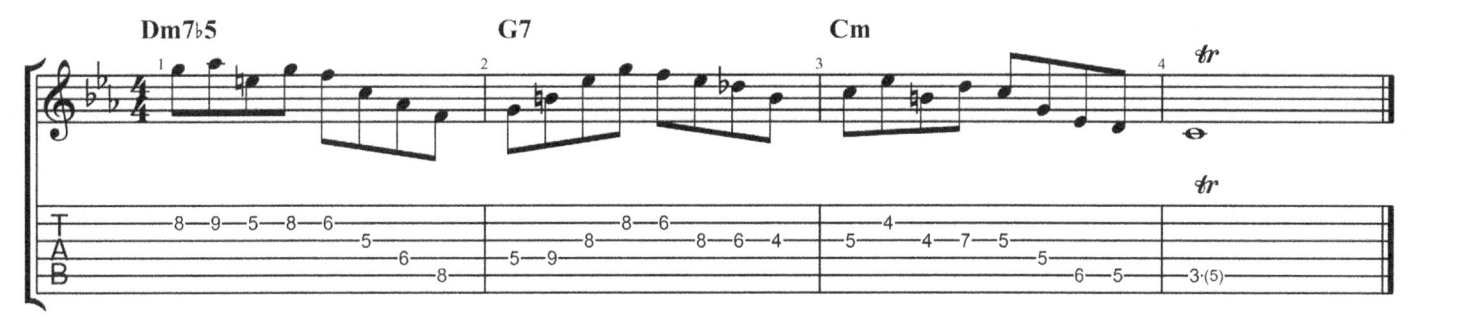

Here is a flowing 1/8th note line. In bar one, C Natural Minor is used over the Dm7b5 chord, then we switch to C Melodic Minor for bars 3-4.

Example 2z21

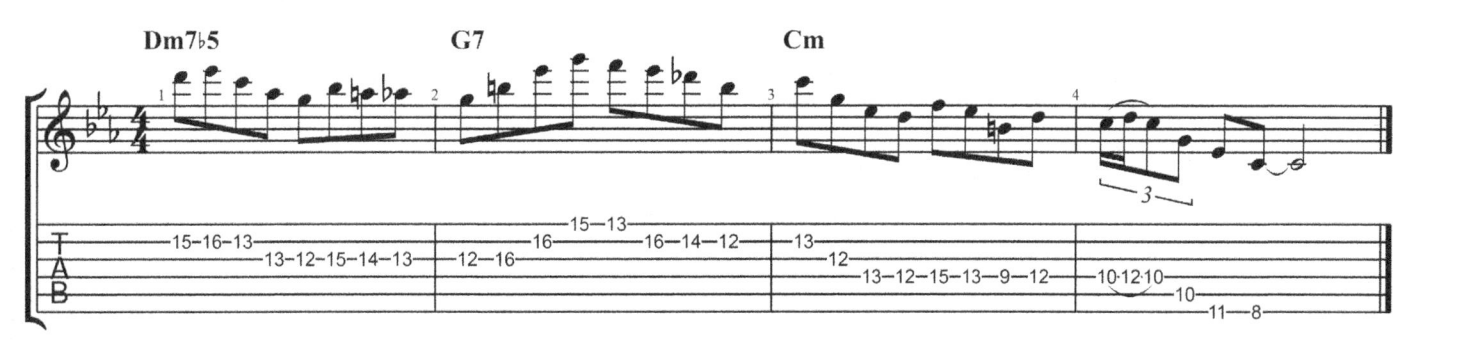

For the next example, let's change things up with a more intervallic approach in the opening bar. Bar one is the C Natural Minor scale, but with a passing E note added.

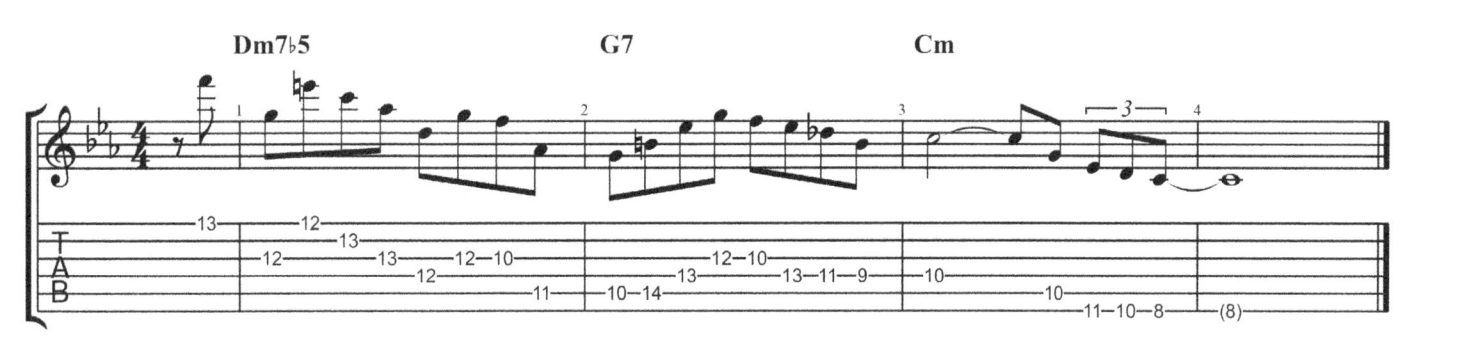

Example 2z22

For the next line we're playing G Whole Tone in a sequenced pattern in bar one, continuing into the cell in bar two. Bar three mimics the phrasing of bar one using the C Melodic Minor scale.

Example 2z23

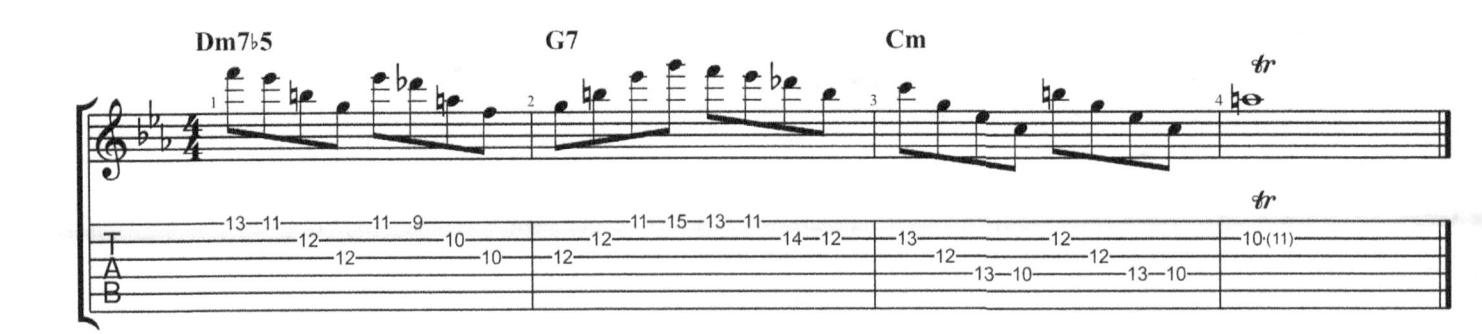

Next, five lines that use Cell 2, starting from the 3rd (B).

In this first line, the B note of the cell is anticipated, and actually falls at the end of bar one, then a rest further breaks up the phrasing.

Example 2z24

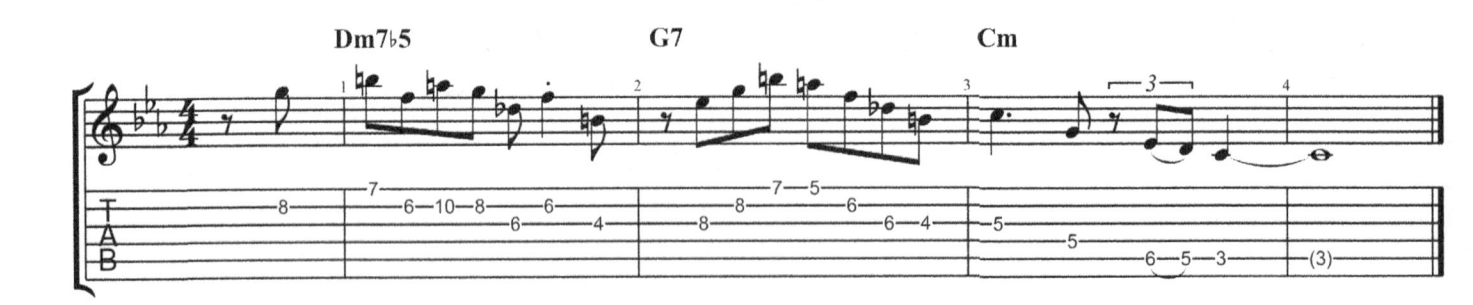

The next example uses an E passing note again in bar one to augment the C Natural Minor scale. The cell in bar two resolves to the b3 of C minor via a whole step.

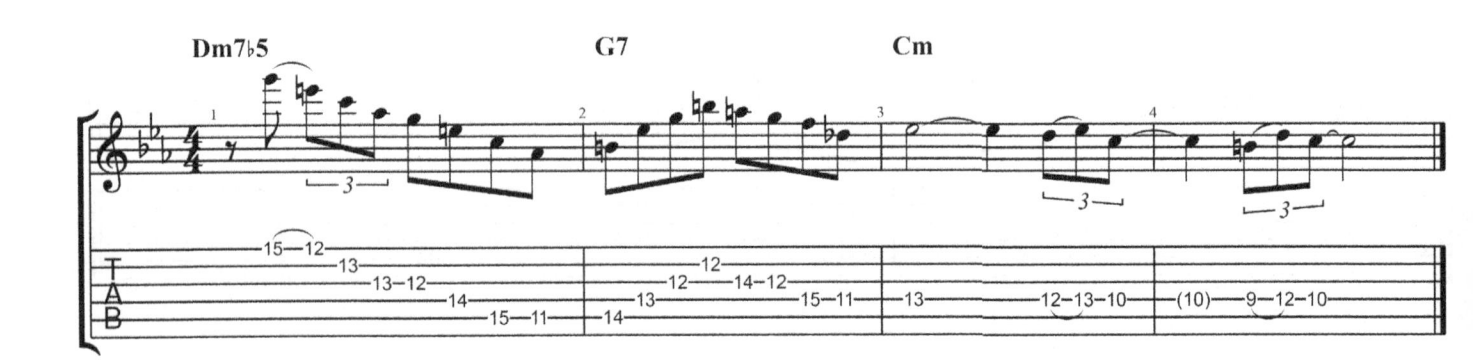

Example 2z25

The lick that opens the next example uses the same idea of adding an E passing note, but also includes a Db/C# note at the end, borrowed from G Whole Tone, to anticipate the cellular phrase in bar two.

Example 2z26

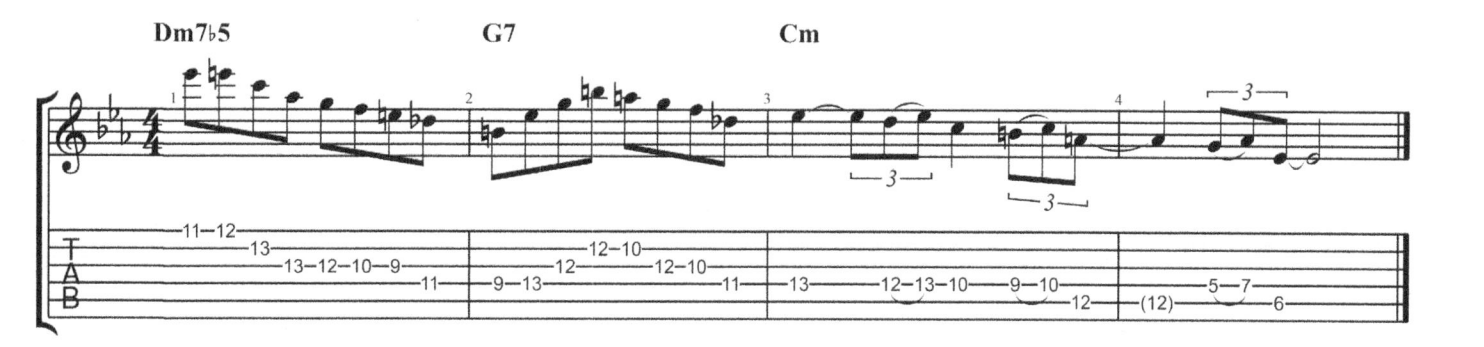

Example 2z27 has a displaced octave idea at the beginning of bar one (octaves played with the notes sounding separately, not together *a la* Wes Montgomery/Pat Martino). Again, the Db/C# of G Whole Tone anticipates the cell in bar two, which is embellished with a triplet figure in the middle.

Example 2z27

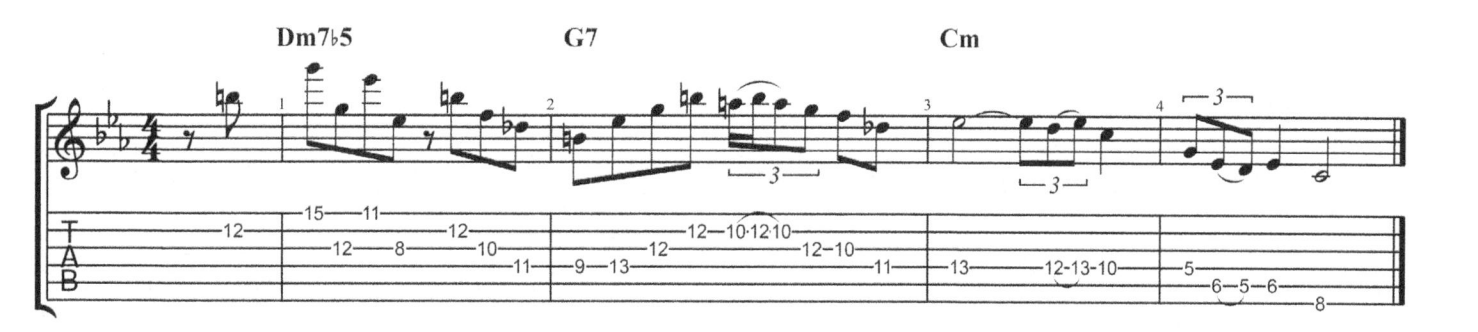

The intervallic opening of this line contrasts with the stable cellular form in the middle. Bar one is G Whole Tone, but with an Ab note borrowed from C Natural Minor.

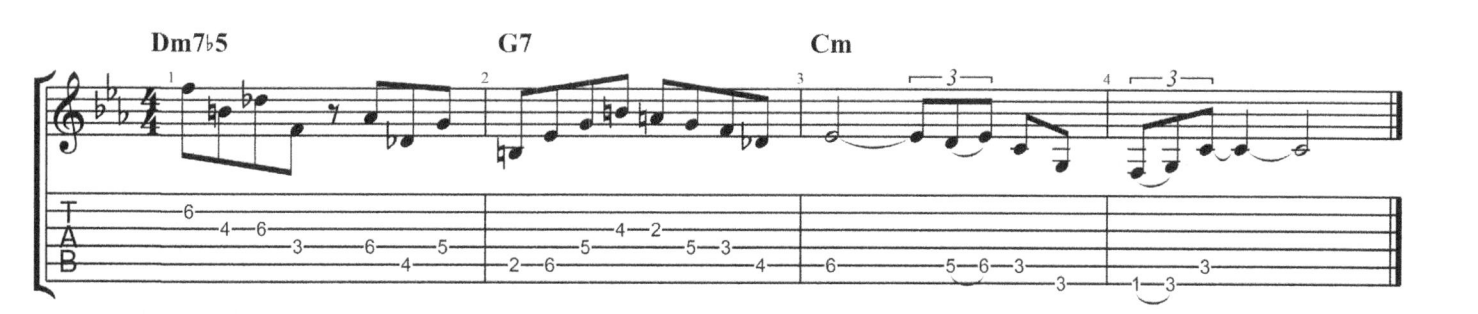

Example 2z28

Now it's time to learn five lines that use Cell 3, launching from the #5 of the dominant chord (notated as Eb as we're in the key of C Minor).

This first example leads with the E note again in bar one. Over the Dm7b5 chord, it has the effect of implying a Dm9b5 sound. The first five notes here are a type of enclosure that targets the F chord tone on beat 3 (Dm7b5 is constructed D F Ab C).

Example 2z29

This time, the E note at the end of bar one is simply a chromatic approach note that targets the first note of the cell in bar two from a half step above.

Example 2z30

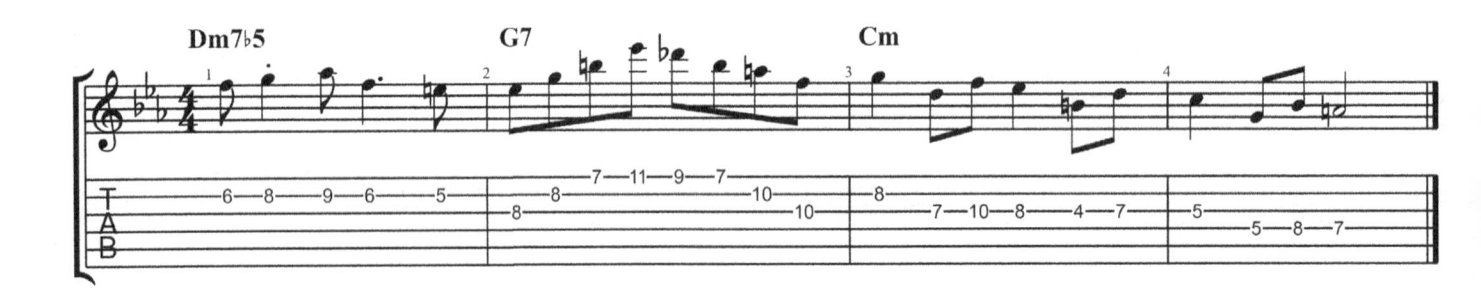

Listen to the audio of the next line carefully before playing it. I punctuated it with rests to break up the rhythm. The rest in bar two falls exactly on beat 3, which is unusual.

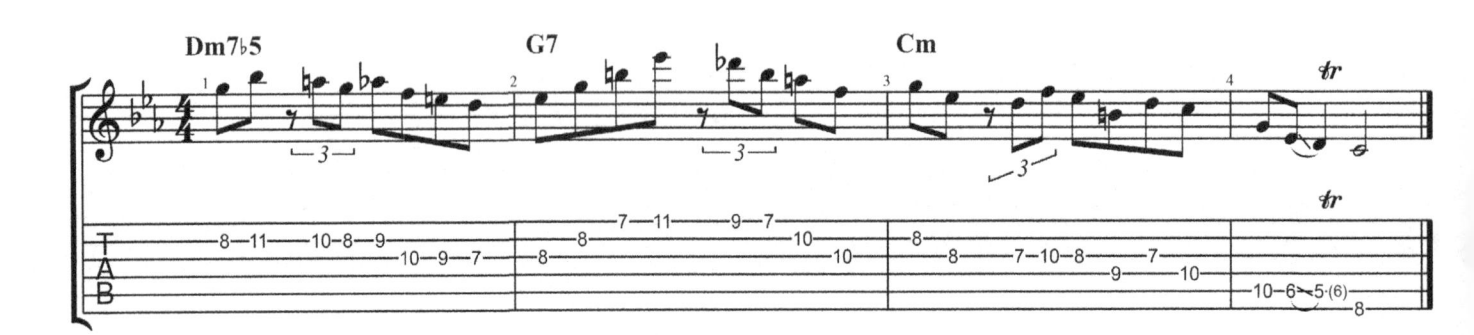

Example 2z31

Here's another intervallic idea that pushes the sound toward contemporary jazz rather than bebop. In bar one, each pair of notes represents a different interval (a 4th, then a 6th, etc).

Example 2z32

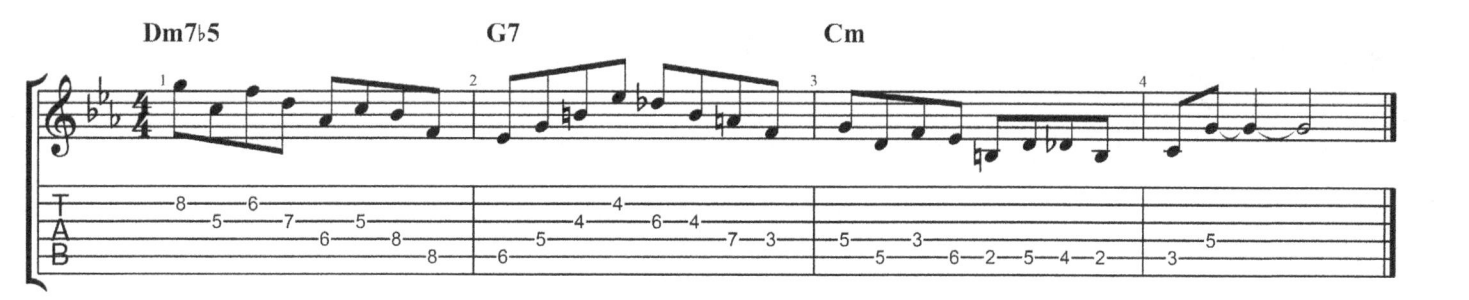

This next line mixes 1/16th note triplets with 1/8th notes in bar one to embellish the descending run. The ascending run over the C minor chord in bars 3-4 uses the C Melodic Minor scale, sequenced into intervals. The first three notes are 4ths; all the rest are 3rds.

Example 2z33

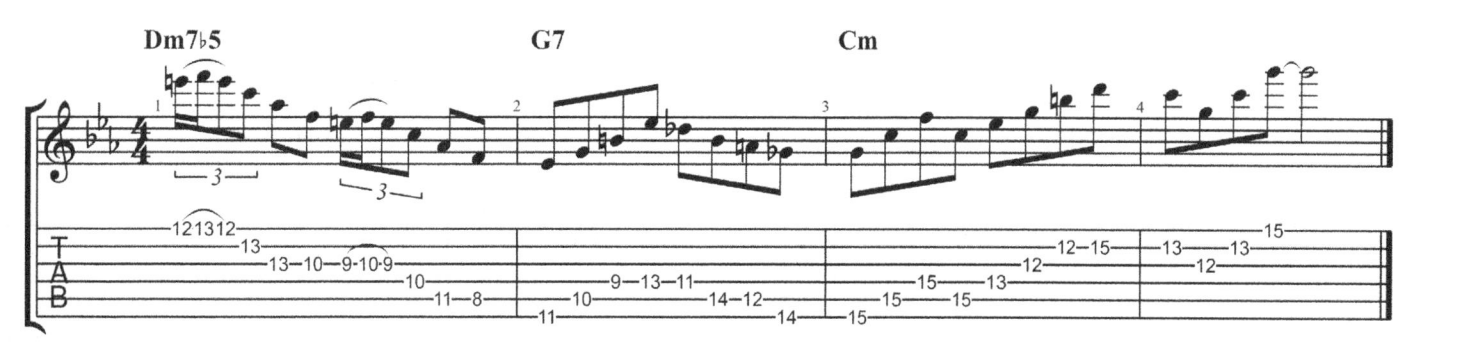

And to close out this chapter, five minor ii V i lines using Cell 4, from the b7 (F) of G7.

Here's a line that uses similar phrasing throughout.

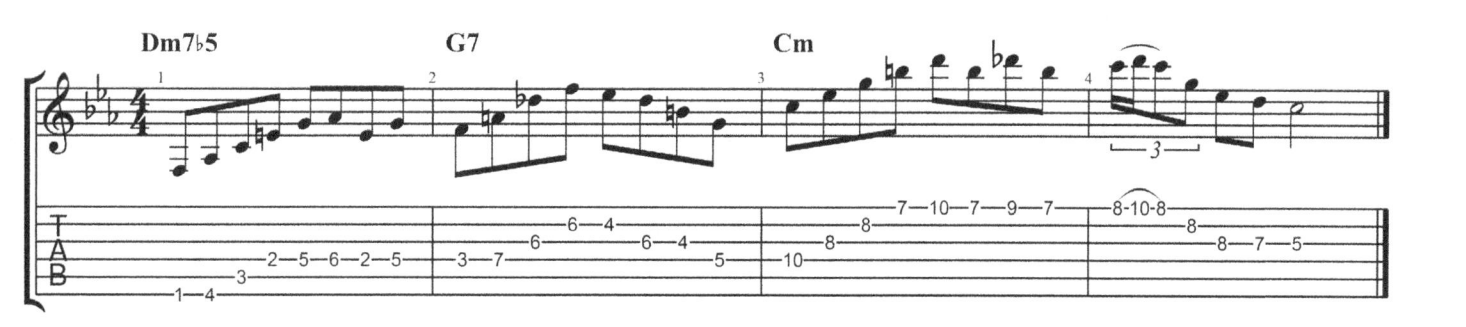

Example 2z34

Here's another modern sounding line. Bar one uses passing notes around the C Melodic Minor scale.

Example 2z35

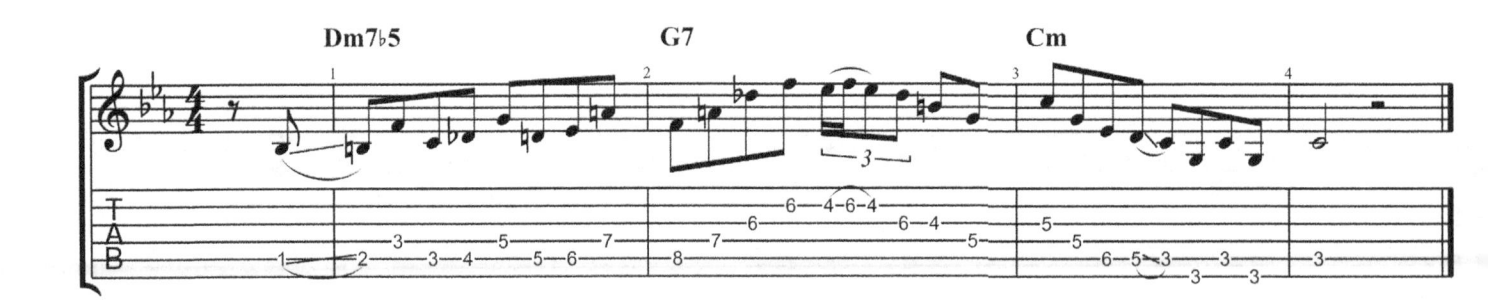

Next, another line that exploits the scale intervals to avoid playing something linear. Bar one uses the G Whole Tone scale over Dm7b5, with string skipping to create wider intervals. In bars 3-4, the three-note repeating phrase is built from C Melodic Minor and the triplet arrangement is designed to rub against the swinging groove.

Example 2z36

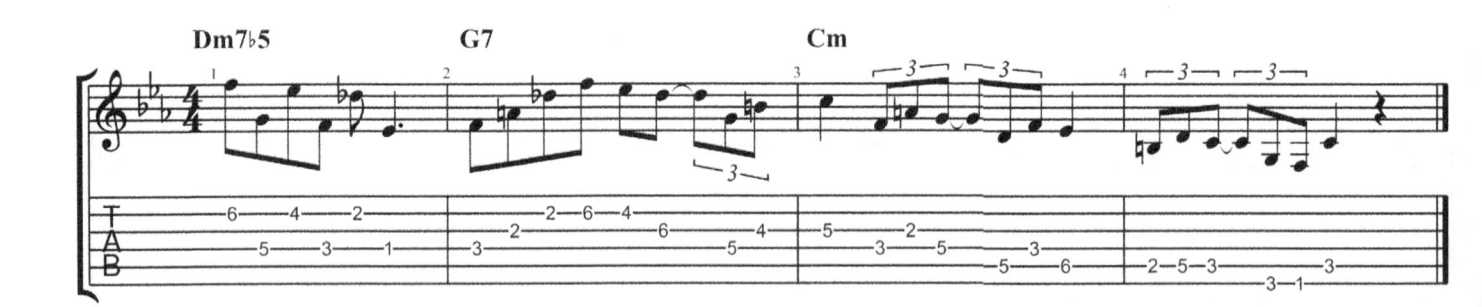

Triplet trills provide the rhythmic interest in this line.

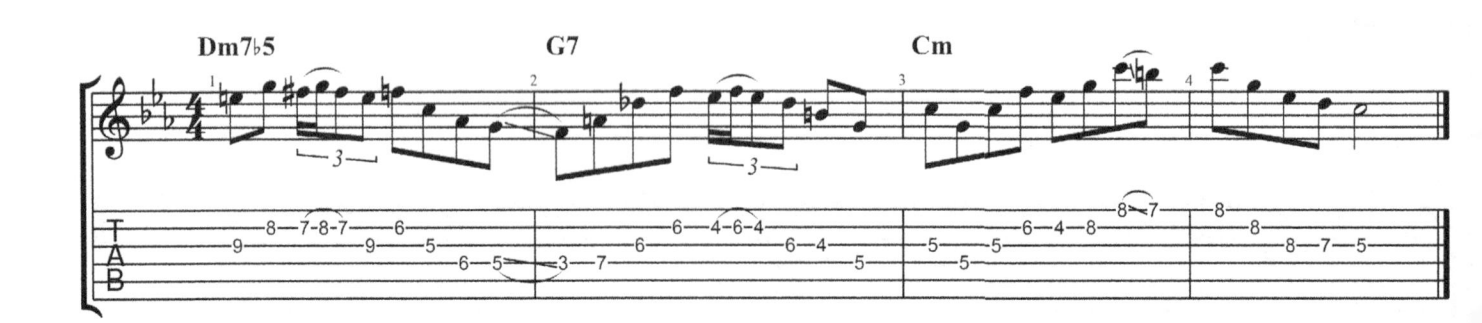

Example 2z37

And to end this chapter, another line "interrupted" by rests to give the phrase a more staccato feel.

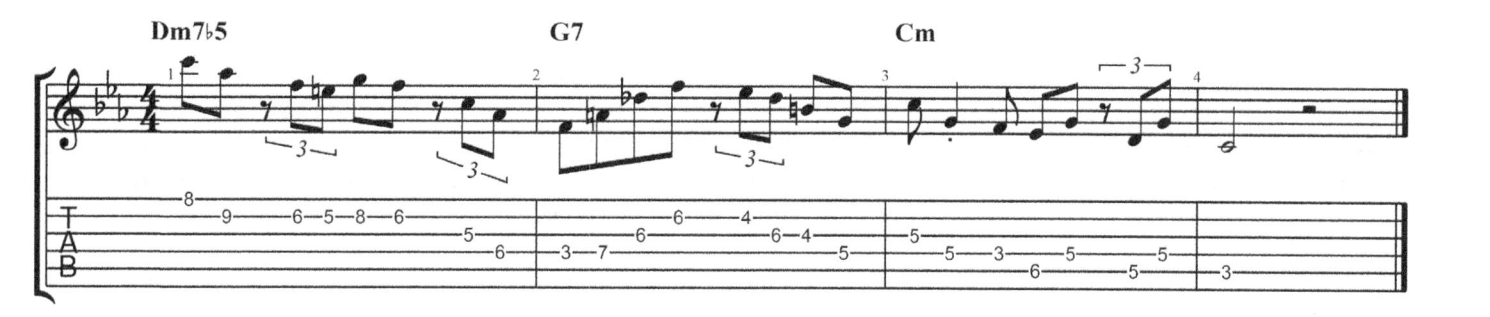

Example 2z38

Chapter Three – Diminished Scale Cells

The Diminished scale produces a darker color than other altered scales and contains some interesting tension notes that will challenge your ears if you're not used to hearing them. It's the jazziest sounding of the scales we're looking at and has been used extensively by musicians like John Coltrane and Allan Holdsworth.

Whenever I teach Diminished scale vocabulary to students, I often find I need to take a step back and explain in basic terms what the scale is and how it's formed. There seems to be a lot of confusion about this scale, not least because there are several different names for it, all of which describe the same thing from a different viewpoint (e.g. Half-Whole Diminished, Whole-Half Diminished, Dominant Diminished, etc).

Here is an easy way to form the diminished scale and know how to apply it. This is the rule jazz musicians use to quickly locate and play the diminished sound over any dominant chord:

Play the diminished scale a half step above the root of a dominant chord.

Take a look at the Ab diminished chord diagram below. You're probably familiar with this common moveable shape for playing it, which has the root note on the first string.

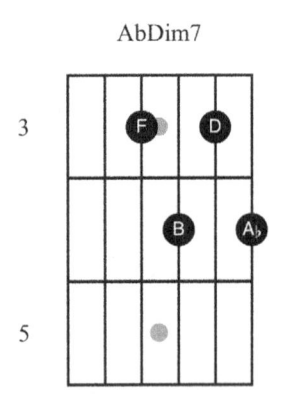

AbDim7

Now, if we add a G bass note to this chord on the sixth string it transforms it into a G7b9:

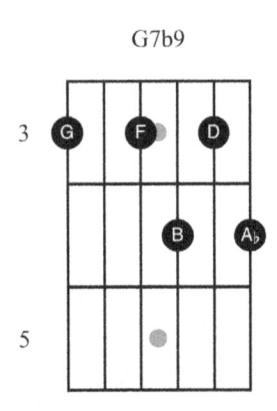

G7b9

48

What I've just demonstrated is known as the *diminished-dominant connection* and illustrates why diminished chords are so closely linked to dominant chords.

Now let's look at how to form the correct scale to play over the G altered dominant chord we've just created. Our starting point is the arpeggio of the Abdim7 chord. Below is an easy way to play it from its root note on the sixth string.

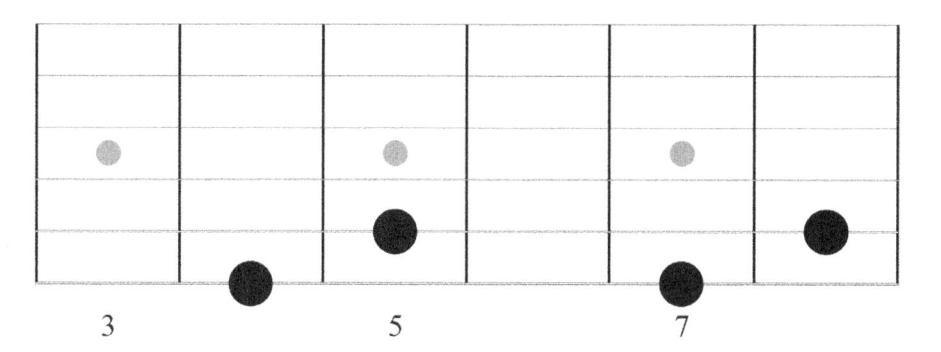

Now, if we add a note a half step below each Abdim7 arpeggio note, we get all eight tones of the Ab Diminished scale but beginning from a G note. Here's how the scale shape looks (the notes we're adding are indicated by hollow circles).

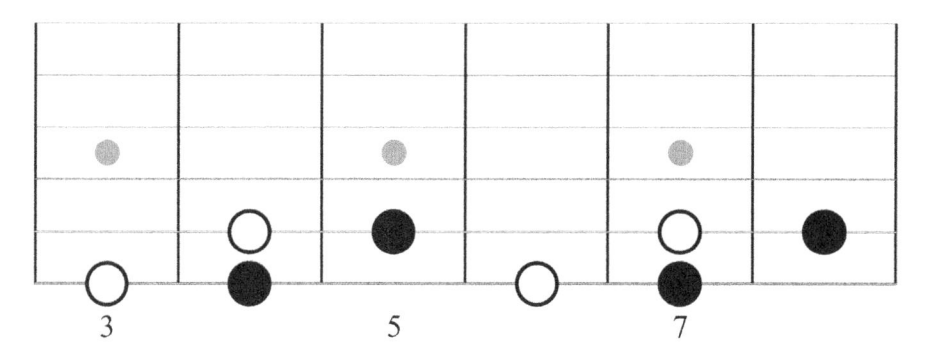

We now have a useful shape for the Ab Diminished scale that begins on the root note of the G7b9 chord. The table below shows the intervals that are highlighted when we play this scale pattern over a *regular* G7 chord.

G	Ab	Bb	B	C#	D	E	F
Root	b9	#9	3rd	#11	5th	13th	b7

The scale contains the root, 3rd, 5th and b7 of G7, plus the b9, #9 and #11 altered tones. It also has an extended 13th interval (E).

Scale shapes

There are several useful shapes for this scale. We'll begin with two three-note-per-string box shapes, then look at two crawling patterns that are useful for spanning the fretboard. Shape 1 is the box shape with a sixth string root.

Shape 1

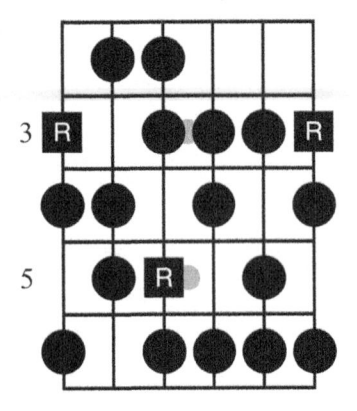

The next three-note-per-string shape has a root on the fifth string. To complete the pattern across the fretboard, I've also indicated the available notes on the sixth string with hollow circles.

Shape 2

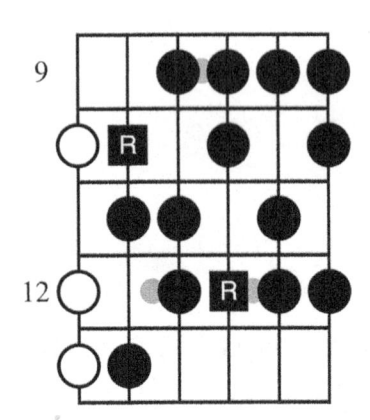

Now check out these four-note-per-string shapes that ascend the neck in a crawling pattern. These shapes are great for quickly covering a wide range of the fretboard and can produce some dynamic results when soloing.

Here is the shape that begins in third position. Notice that it has the same pattern of notes on *every string*, which makes it much easier to memorize.

Shape 3

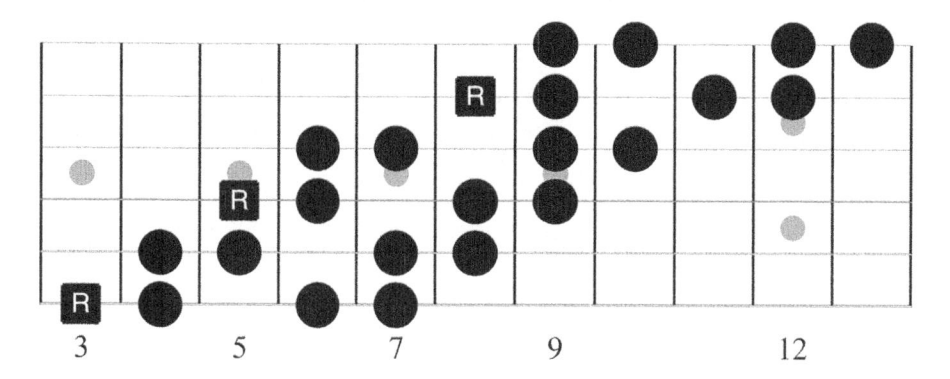

If you find it a stretch to play four notes on one string, especially in the lower register, then you can add a position slide, which is how I always play this pattern. Play the first note on the sixth string 3rd fret with your first finger, then immediately slide up one fret to play the 4th fret also with the first finger. The remaining two notes are played with the third and fourth fingers respectively.

Execute that first finger slide on *every* string. When you've practiced this several times and are comfortable with the slide, you'll find that it facilitates playing the scale at speed.

When descending the scale, do the slide in reverse: play the highest note with the fourth finger, the next note with the third finger, the next with the first finger, then slide down one fret to play the final note of the pattern also with the first finger.

Here is the equivalent shape in the higher register, with the root note on the fifth string.

Shape 4

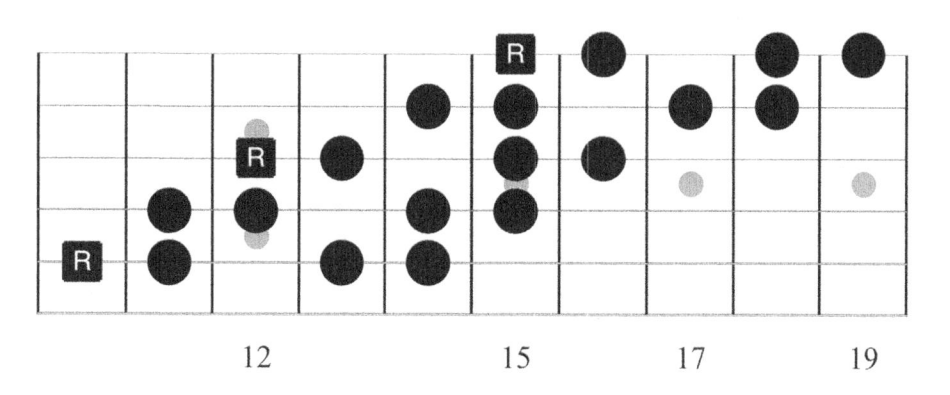

The melodic cells

Now let's move on to look at the four melodic cells we can create using this scale. First of all, we want cells that will resolve from the V to the I chord in the context of the Major ii V I sequence.

51

This time around, we are going to make a small change to Cell 1, which only applies when using the Diminished scale. We want to hear the diminished seventh character of this scale when we play the cell, so instead of beginning Cell 1 from the root note of G7 chord as expected, we'll launch it from the outside sounding Ab note of the scale.

Without this adjustment, the cell sounds too similar to the Mixolydian cell to begin with. Changing to an Ab note means that the cell now begins on the b9 interval and the first three notes spell a diminished triad – which is the sound we want to hear. Check it out:

Example 3a – Cell 1

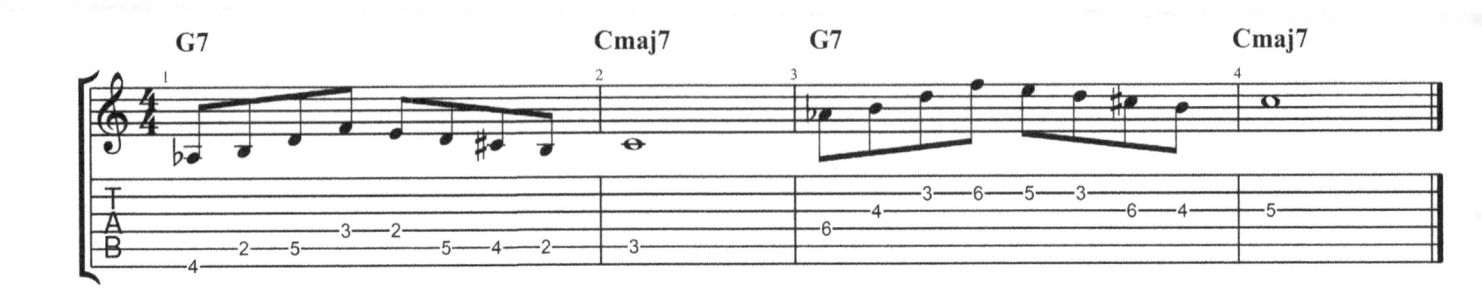

Cell 2 is built from the 3rd (B) of G7.

Example 3b – Cell 2

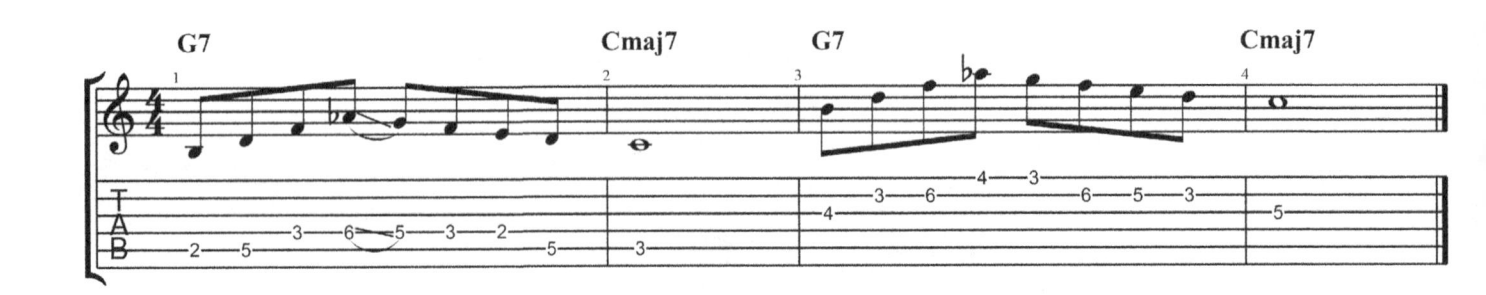

Here is the cell built from the 5th (D) of G7.

Example 3c – Cell 3

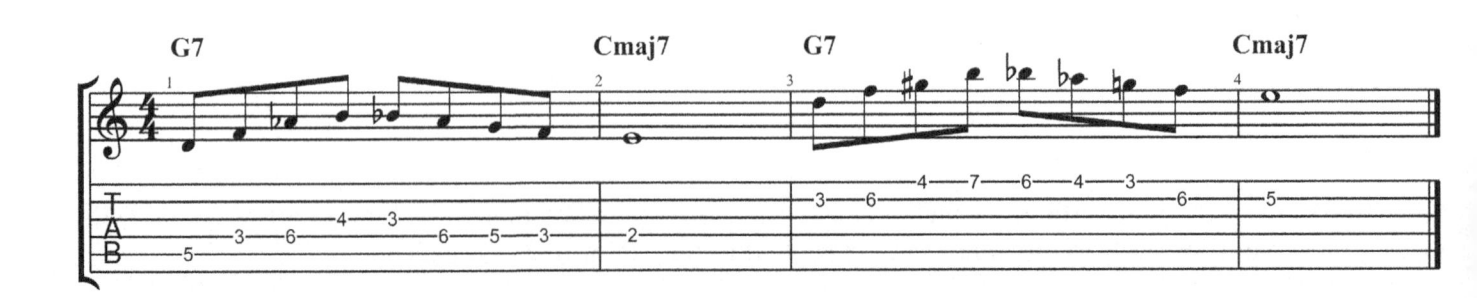

And Cell 4, from the b7 (F).

Example 3d – Cell 4

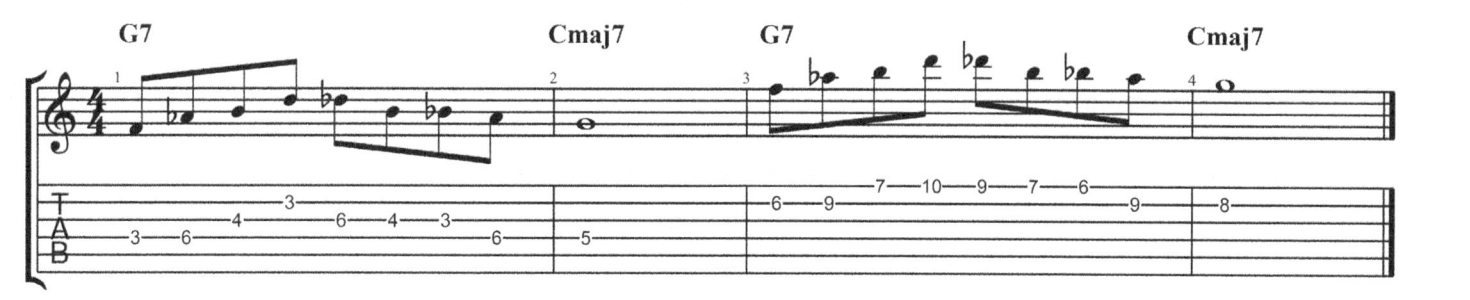

Putting the cells into a Major ii V I

With our four melodic cells in place, it's time to hear them in the context of the Major ii V I with some simple 1/8th note lines. First, here are two lines that use Cell 1, launched from the b9 (Ab). I've included a couple of passing notes over the Dm7 chord to spice things up a little more.

Example 3e

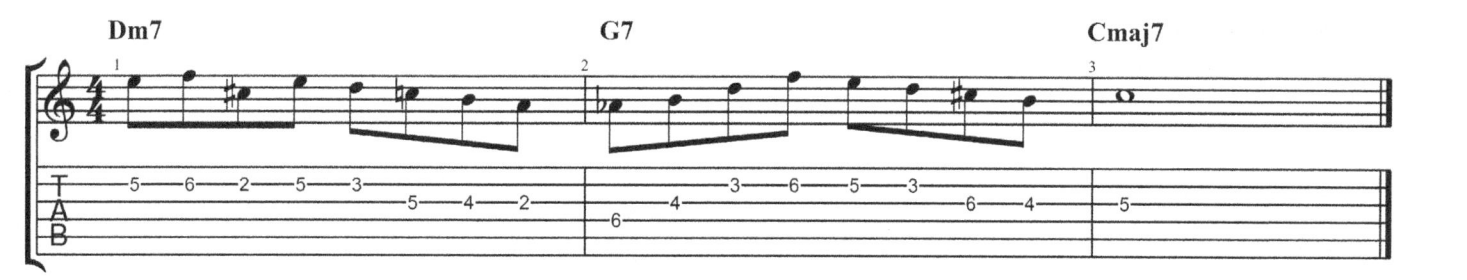

Example 3f

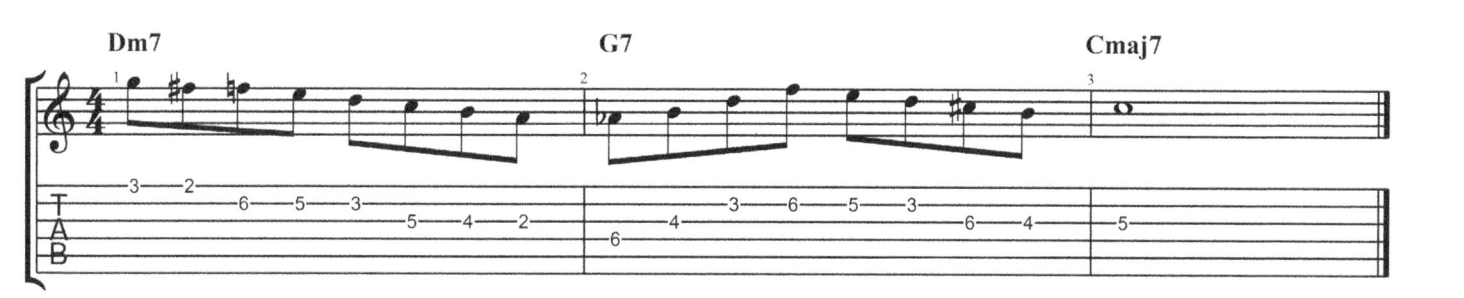

Next, two lines that use Cell 2, from the 3rd (B).

Example 3g

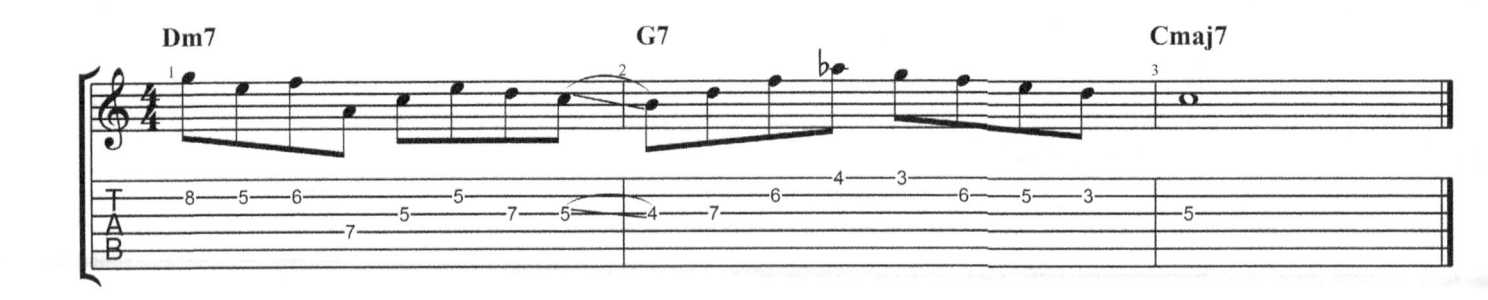

Example 3h

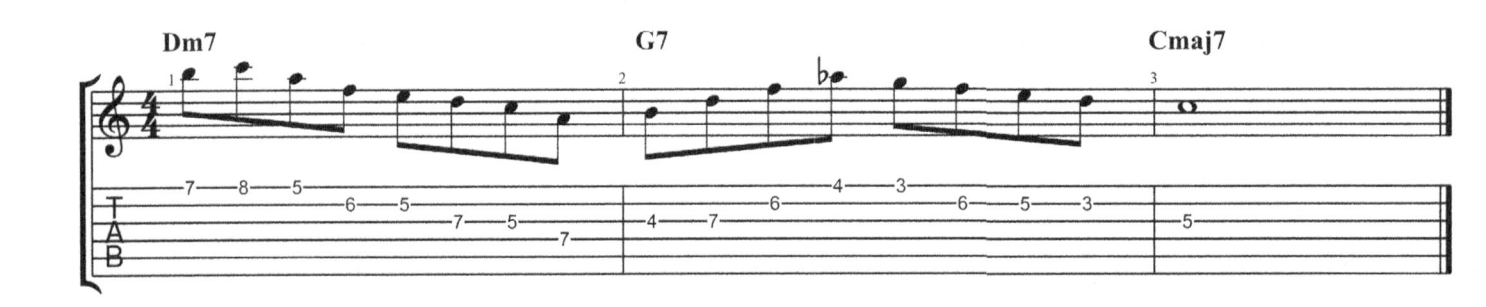

Now, two lines that use Cell 3 from the 5th (D).

Example 3i

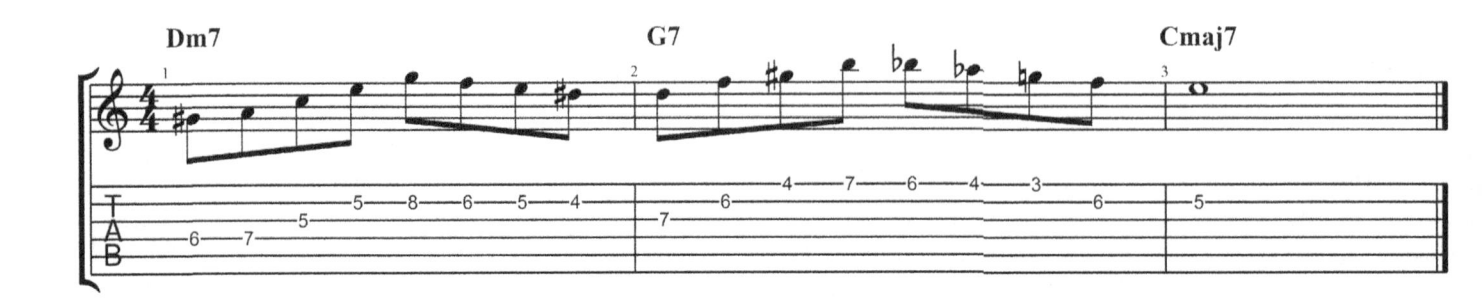

54

Example 3j

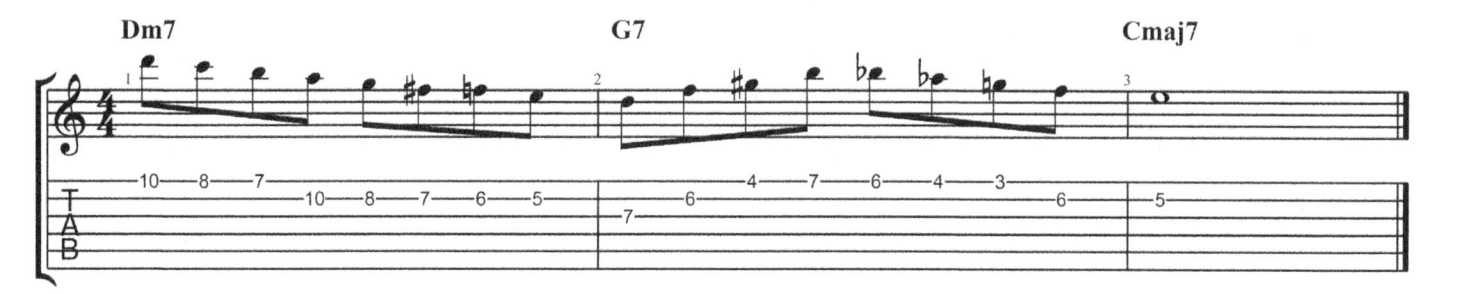

And here are two lines constructed using Cell 4 from the b7 (F).

Example 3k

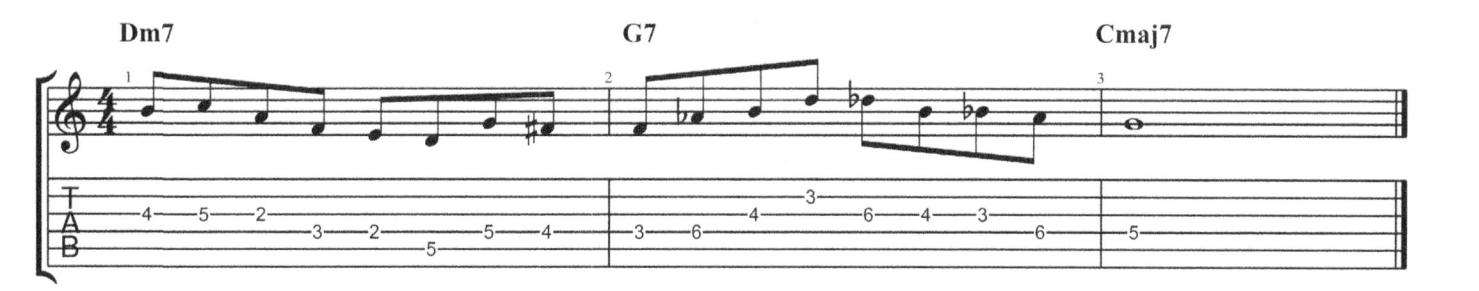

Example 3l

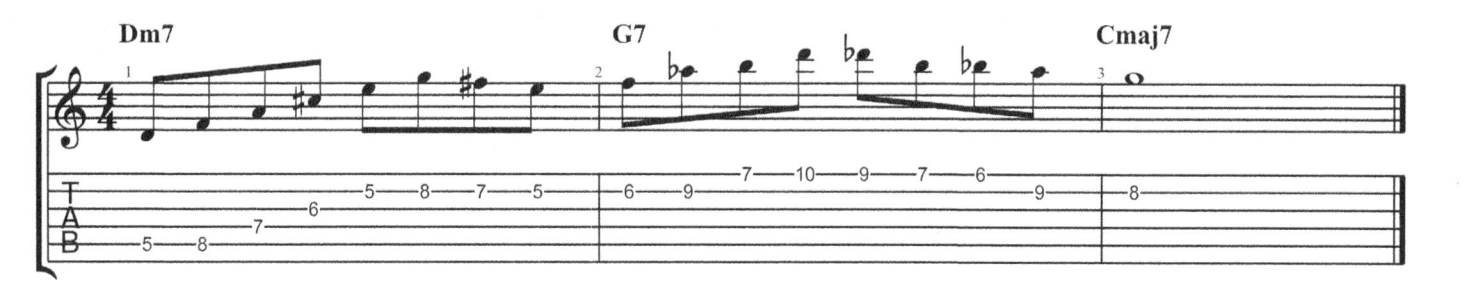

More advanced cellular vocabulary

Now we get to have some fun with our diminished scale cells as we use them to build more creative jazz lines – firstly over the Major ii V I sequence.

In this first example, after playing a straight 1/8th note line in bar one using the C Major scale, the cell is broken up with a triplet embellishment. Then the phrasing over Cmaj7 in bars 3-4 is more intervallic.

Example 3m

Example 3n uses the G Half-Whole Diminished scale over the Dm7 chord as well as G7 to create an angular sounding line. All of the scale notes work over Dm7 and represent upper extensions or altered notes. The only note that doesn't truly "fit" is the C# (which is the major 7th, superimposed over the chord's minor 7th) but because the tension is fleeting and quickly resolved, it just sounds like a chromatic passing note.

Example 3n

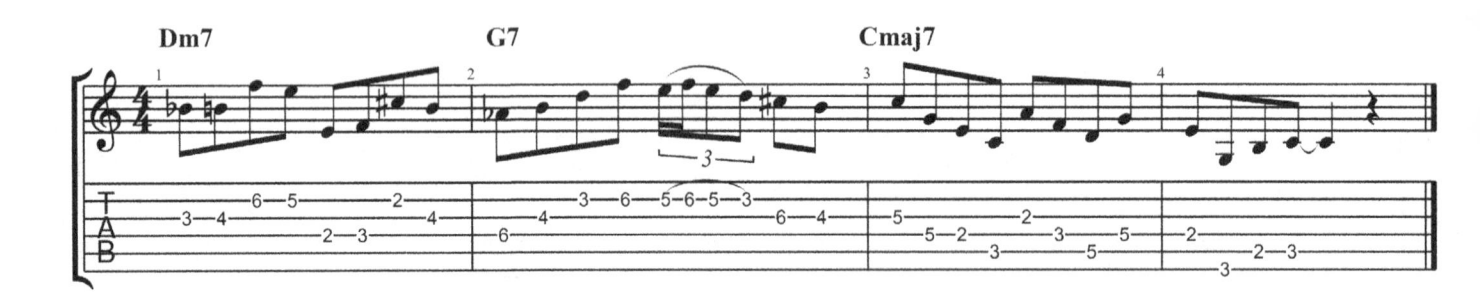

The next example uses a similar strategy, with the diminished scale used again in bar one, but the phrase also contains a non-scale passing A note, which is targeting the b9 (Ab).

Example 3o

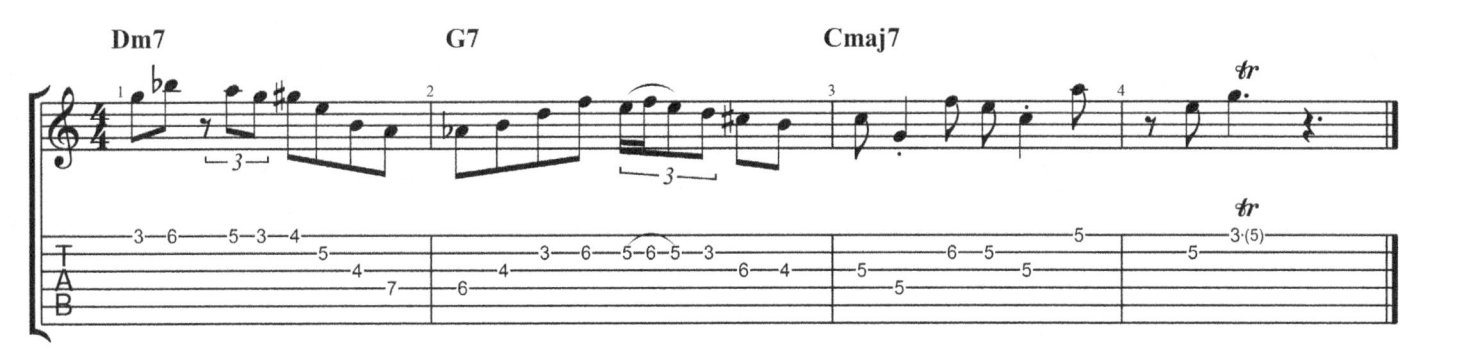

As we've seen with earlier examples, often all a line needs is some strategic rests to grab our attention. Listen to the audio to nail the phrasing on this one.

Example 3p

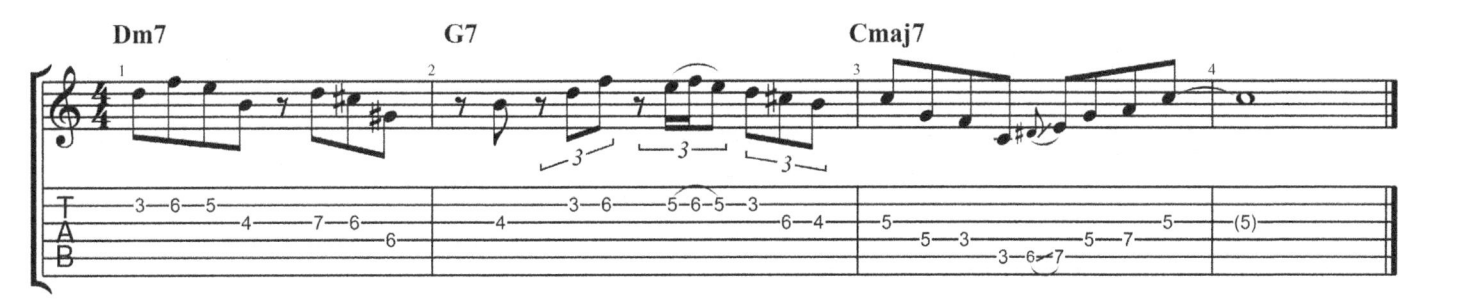

Example 3q also relies on the diminished scale to connect the ascending line of bar one with the cell of bar two.

Example 3q

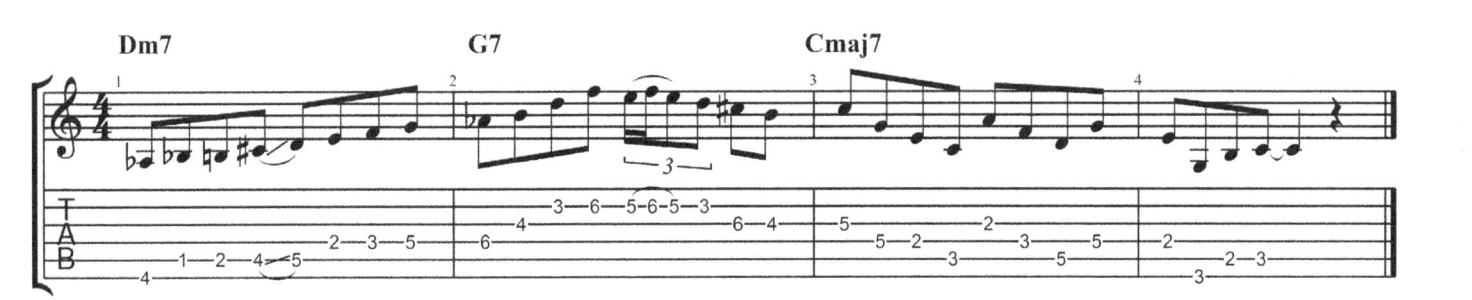

Example 3r uses a diminished scale sequence in bar one, and this phrasing is replicated in bars 3-4.

Example 3r

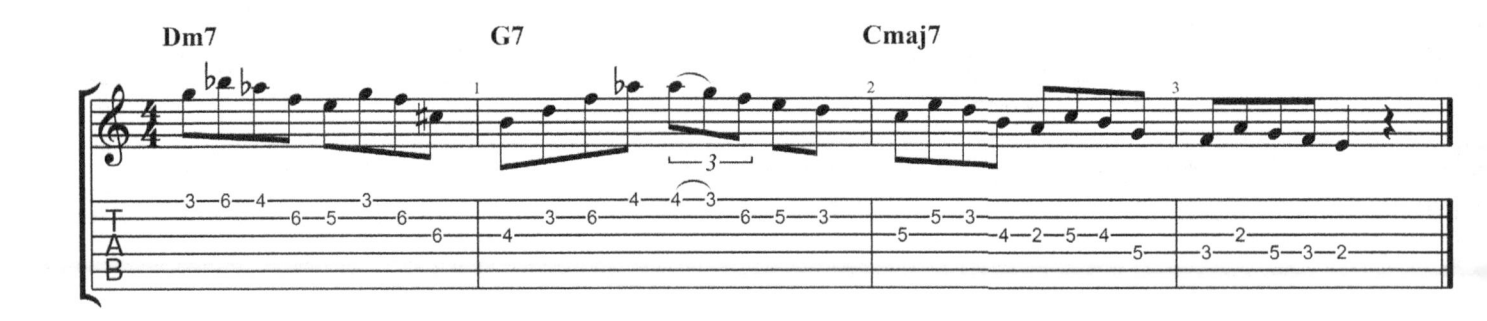

The next example has a similar opening line but with some subtle variation and a different sequencing idea over the Cmaj7 chord.

Example 3s

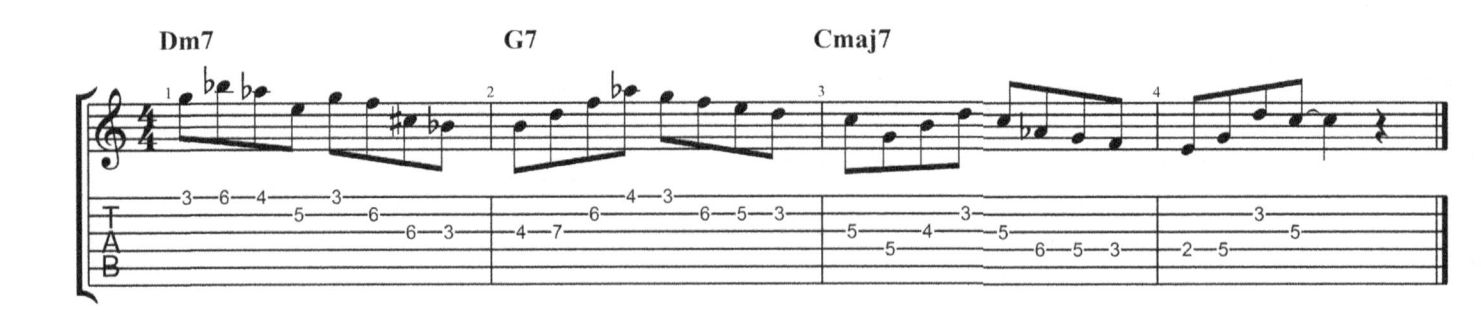

Here's a different kind of idea in bar one. Study the shape of the line and you'll see that the idea is to descend chromatically on the second string. Some notes are C Major scale tones while others are chromatic passing notes. The phrase ends on a C note so that it can resolve a half step to the first note of the dominant chord cell.

Example 3t

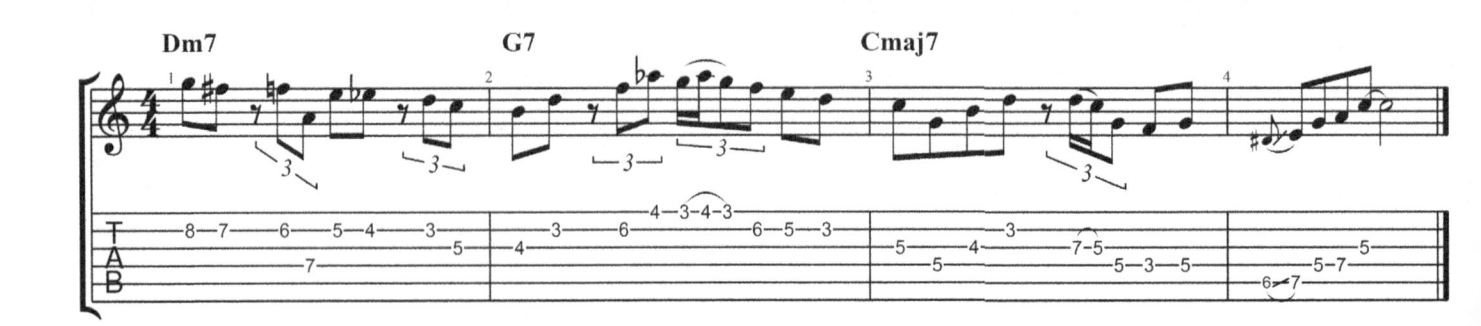

The next line creates a cascading effect by using 2nd intervals from the diminished scale in bar one. The C note at the end of the bar is not from G Half-Whole Diminished but is a passing note to resolve to the dominant chord cell, like the previous example. In bars 3-4, chromatic approach notes are used in enclosures that target C Major scale tones.

Example 3u

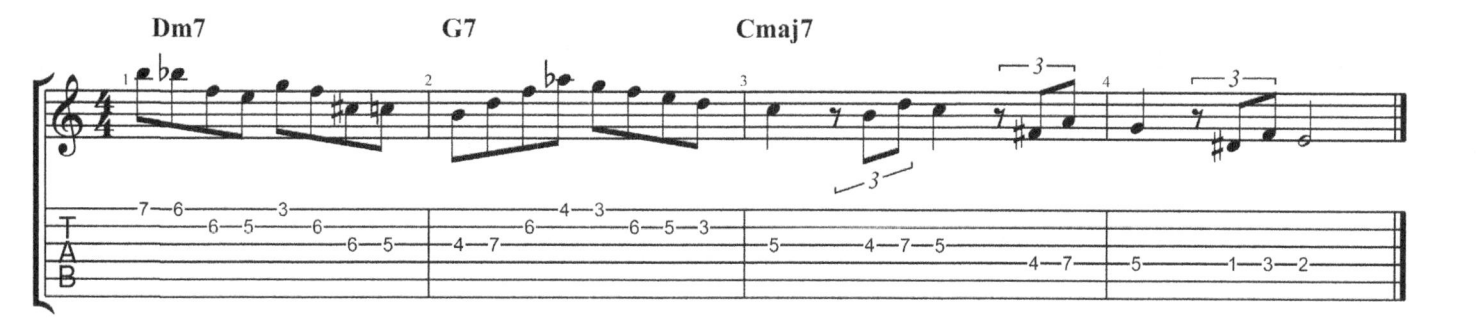

Here is another diminished scale sequence in bar one that creates an ascending lick that snakes its way up into the cell.

Example 3v

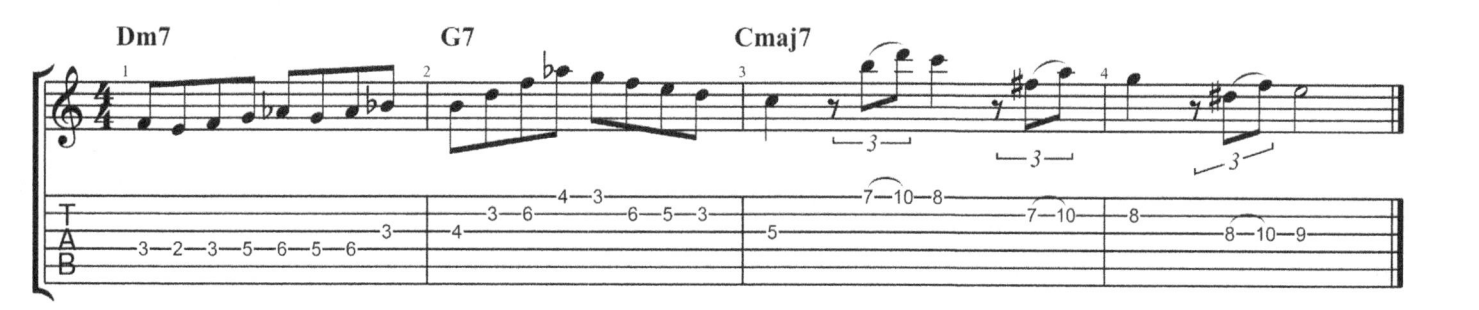

Now let's move on to five lines using Cell 3, from the 5th (D) of G7.

In bar one, a simple C Major scale run ends with a chromatic Eb which resolves a half step to the D note that begins the cell. Check out the audio, as this kind of swinging line needs to be played slightly behind the beat to capture the feel.

Example 3w

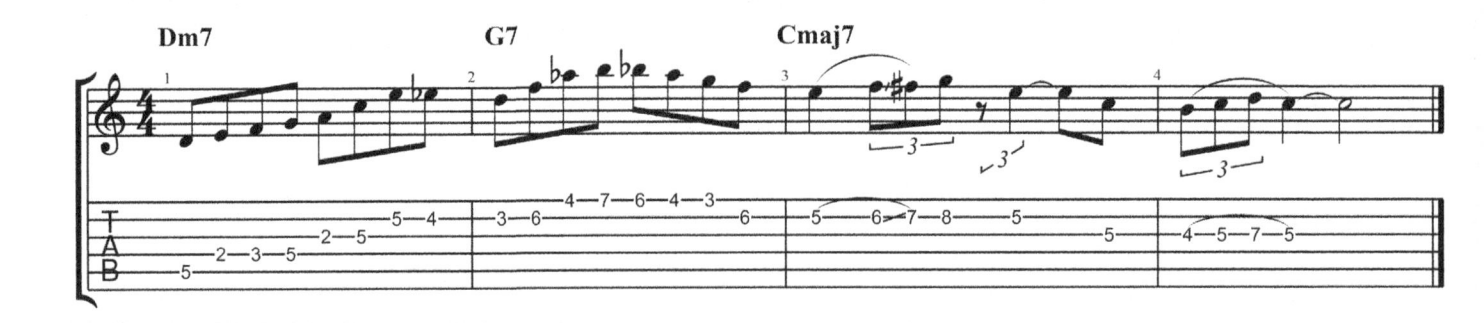

[Musical notation and tablature over Dm7 - G7 - Cmaj7 progression]

The next example uses G Half-Whole Diminished over the Dm7 chord and resolves to Cell 3 with a whole step movement.

Example 3x

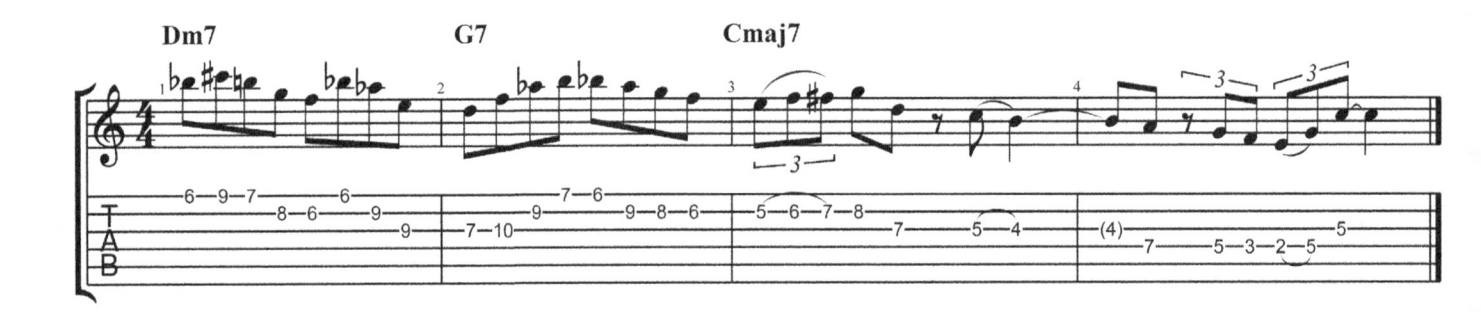

[Musical notation and tablature over Dm7 - G7 - Cmaj7 progression]

Often, good phrasing is about finding one key idea and repeating it. In this line, the idea is to play an 1/8th note phrase that begins with a straight 1/8th followed by 1/8th note triplets. The idea in bar one is repeated in bar three.

Example 3y

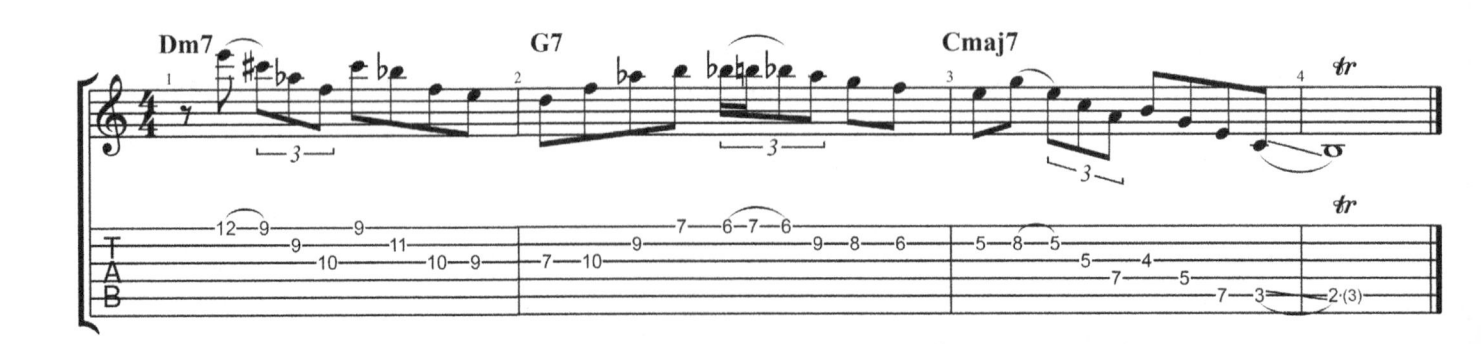

[Musical notation and tablature over Dm7 - G7 - Cmaj7 progression]

In bar one of Example 3z, the first four notes are from G Half-Whole Diminished. In the second four notes, a non-scale tone (Eb) is introduced to give the phrase an outside-inside feel. (Over a Dm7 chord, Eb creates the sound of the more colorful Dm7b9).

Example 3z

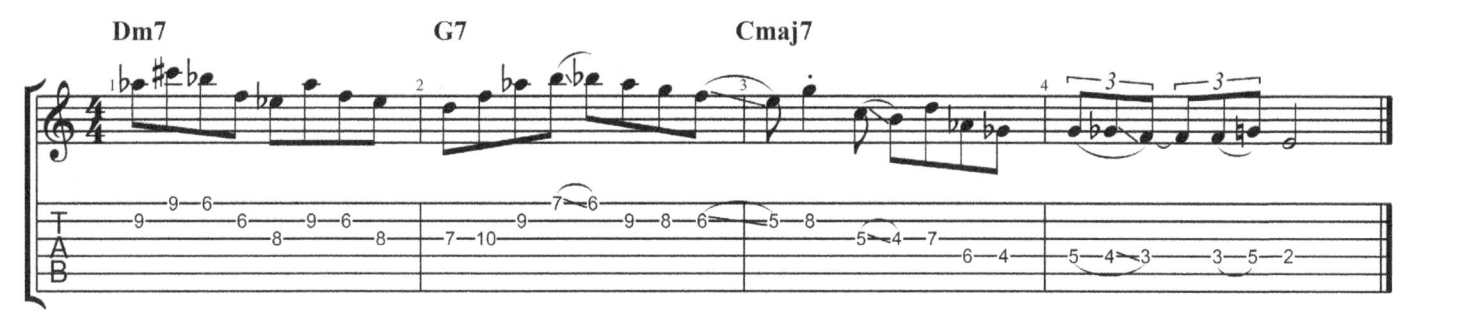

By superimposing the diminished scale over the ii chord rather than using the parent scale of the key, it's possible to create lines with much more color, such as this descending run.

Example 3z1

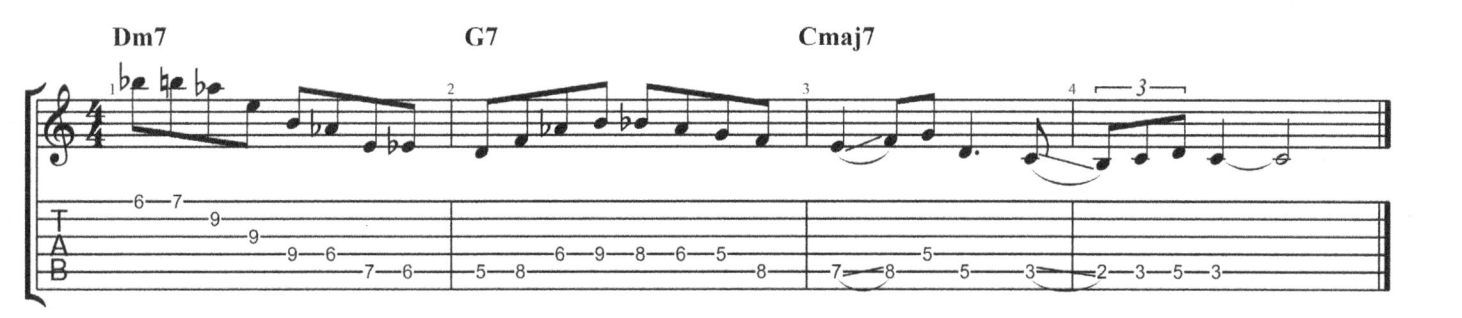

Next up, five example lines that use Cell 4, starting from the b7 (F) of G7.

In bar two, a triplet breaks up the cell phrasing and resolves to the 5th (G) of the Cmaj7 chord.

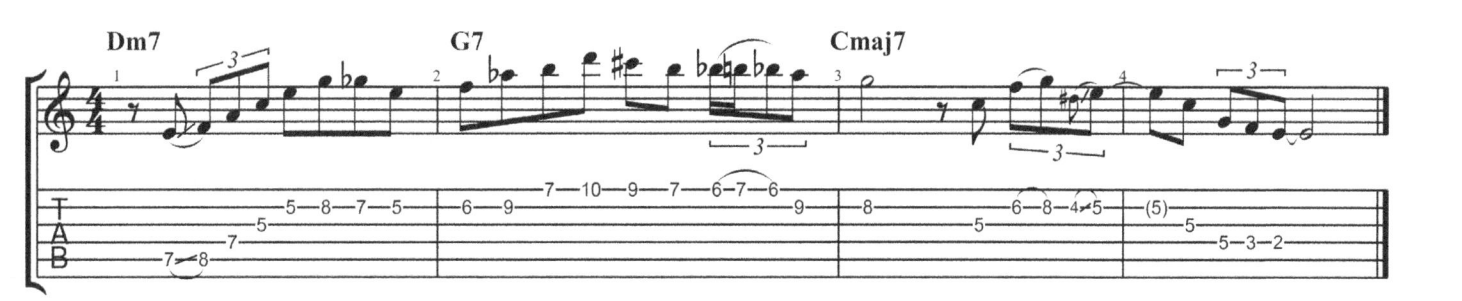

Example 3z2

The next example begins with an intervallic string-skipping idea, using G Half-Whole Diminished over the Dm7 chord. If you can incorporate ideas like this into your jazz vocabulary, it will immediately set you apart as a player who has something different to offer. Keep your fingering and note separation nice and clean when playing the skipping intervals. The rest of this line is broken up with lots of triplet phrases.

Example 3z3

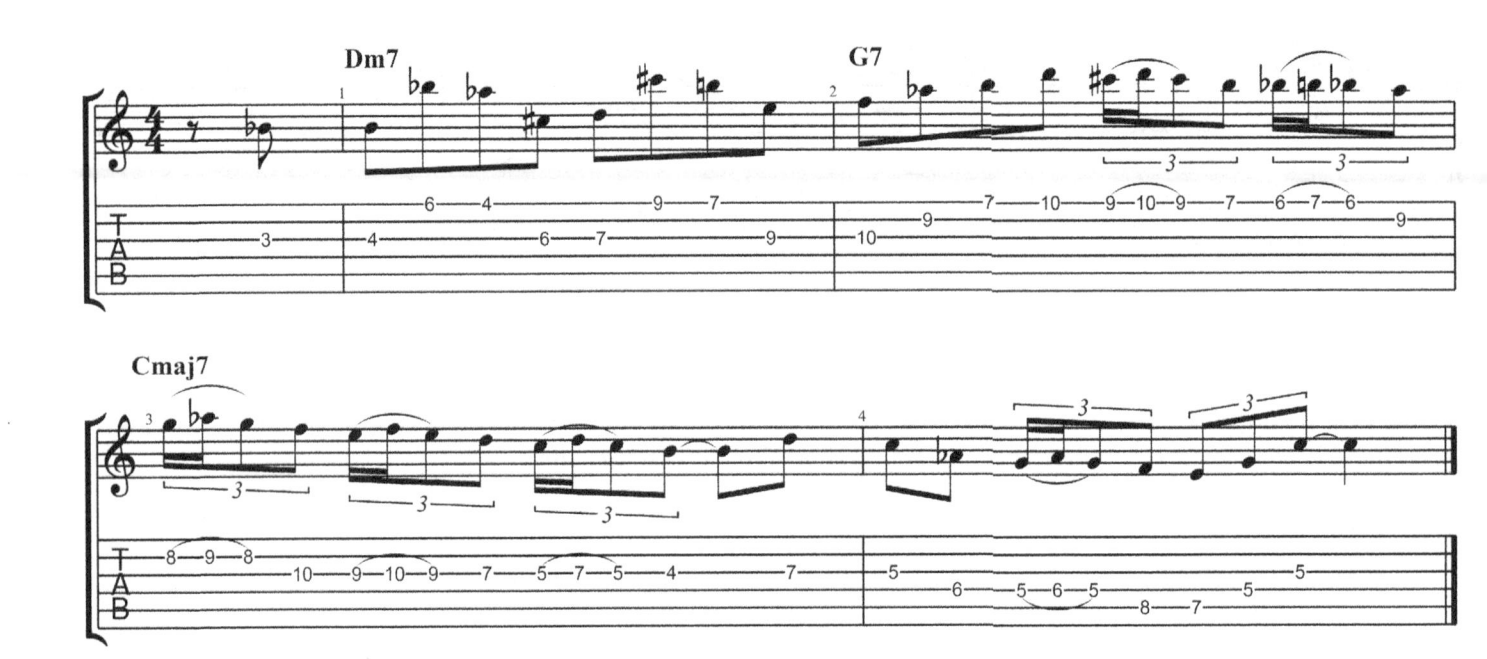

This line uses the diminished scale to create a short motif in bar one, ending with a passing note to resolve a half step to the cell in bar two. There is a variation on the previous lick's triplet phrases in bars 3-4.

Example 3z4

Here's an idea that uses a chromatic run down to transition from bar one to two.

Example 3z5

To end our Major ii V I examples, here's a line that uses consistent phrasing throughout to spell out the chords.

Example 3z6

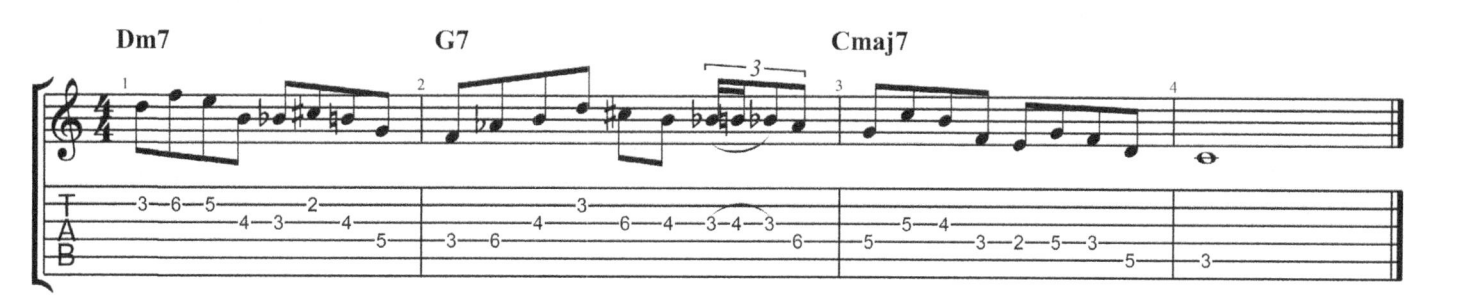

Diminished Melodic Cells in a Minor ii V i

Next, we turn our attention to applying the diminished scale in a minor ii V i context. Here, our chord sequence will be Dm7b5 – G7 – Cm7.

As usual, we'll begin by defining the four melodic cells that will lie at the heart of every melodic line that follows. At this point, however, we need to make a small adjustment.

The G Half-Whole Diminished scale (G Ab Bb B C# D E F) contains an E note, but the parent key of C Minor contains an Eb. Using the diminished scale's E note in the cells sounds odd to my ears, so this is the one and only occasion where I alter a note in the scale to make it fit better.

We've not encountered this problem before, because the G Whole Tone scale contains a D# (Eb) note, and the G Altered scale we'll look at in the next chapter also has an Eb.

So, we only need to make this small adjustment for the diminished scale, and only in the melodic cells themselves. We can play G Half-Whole Diminished over a Dm7 chord, where the E note creates a Dm9b5 sound, no problem – we only want to avoid it over the V to i chord resolution.

Also, remember that Cell 1 begins from the scale's b9 (Ab)!

Example 3z7 – Minor Cell 1

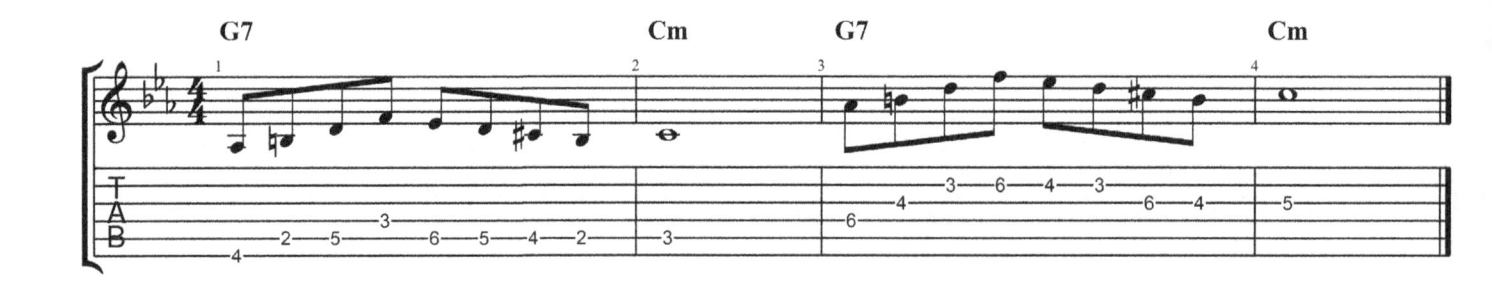

Here's the cell from the 3rd (B).

Example 3z8 – Minor Cell 2

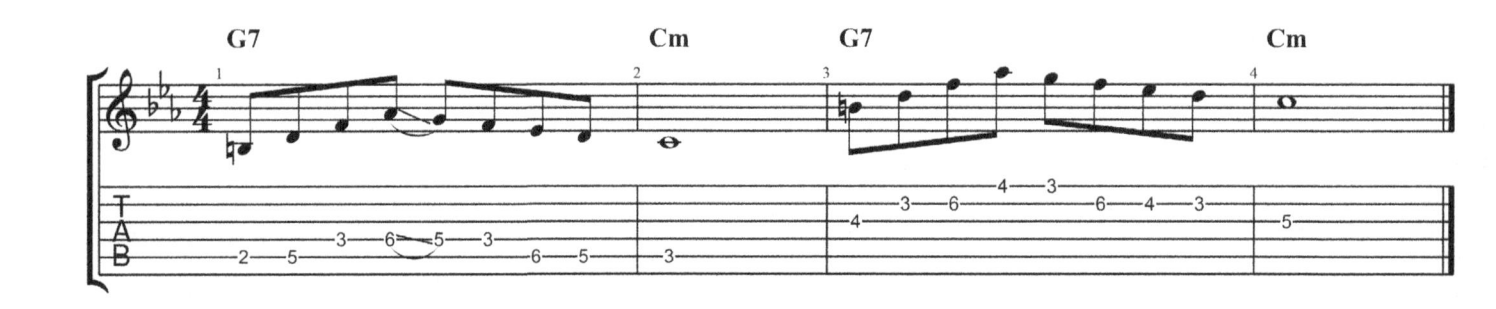

Next, the cell from the 5th (D).

Example 3z9 – Minor Cell 3

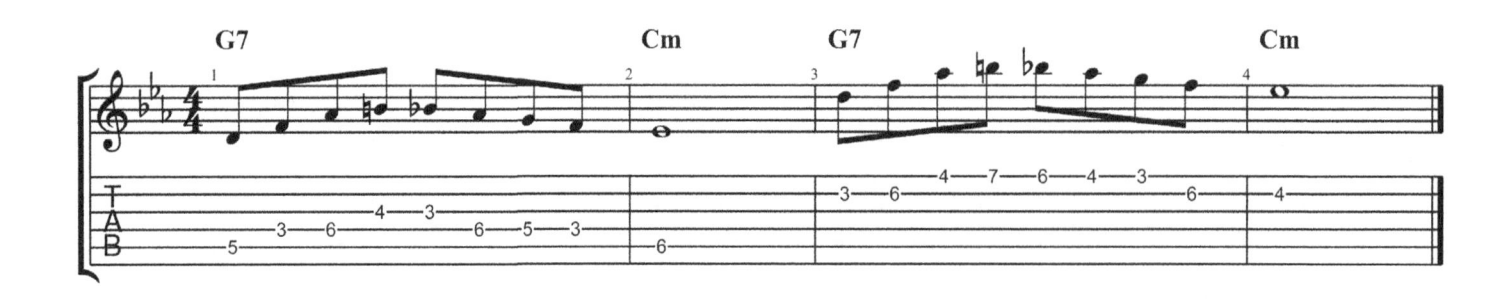

And lastly, the cell from the b7 (F).

Example 3z10 – Minor Cell 4

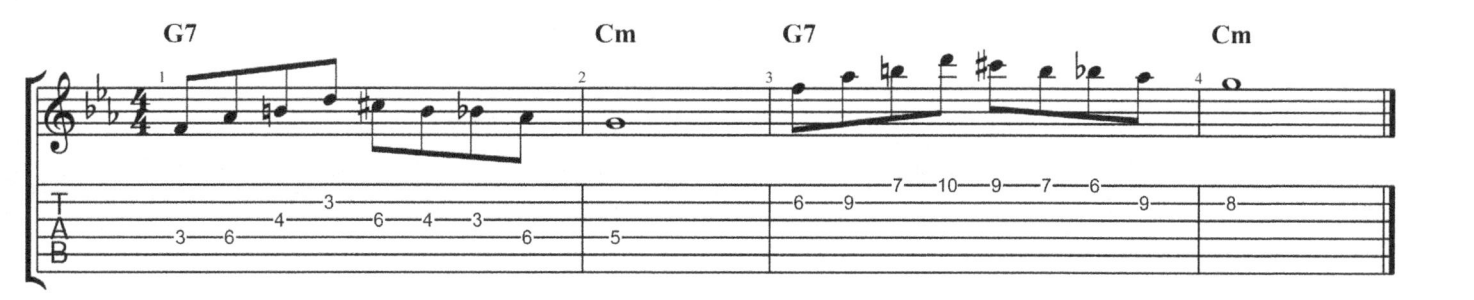

Putting the cells into a Minor ii V I

Now, let's take those cells and practice them in some simple minor ii V i lines.

First, two lines that use Cell 1.

Example 3z11

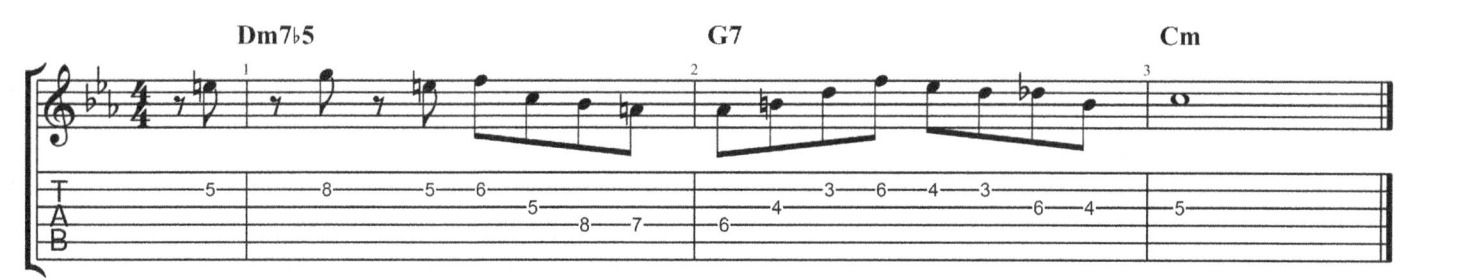

Example 3z12

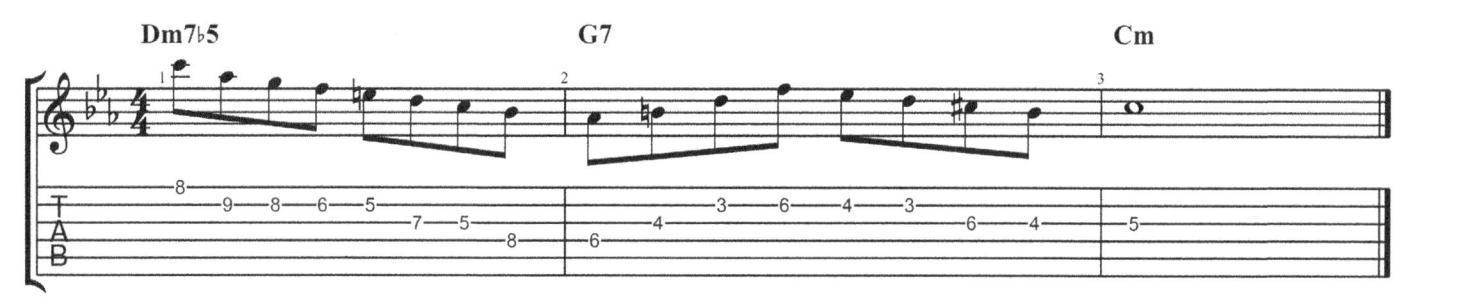

Next, two lines that use Cell 2.

Example 3z13

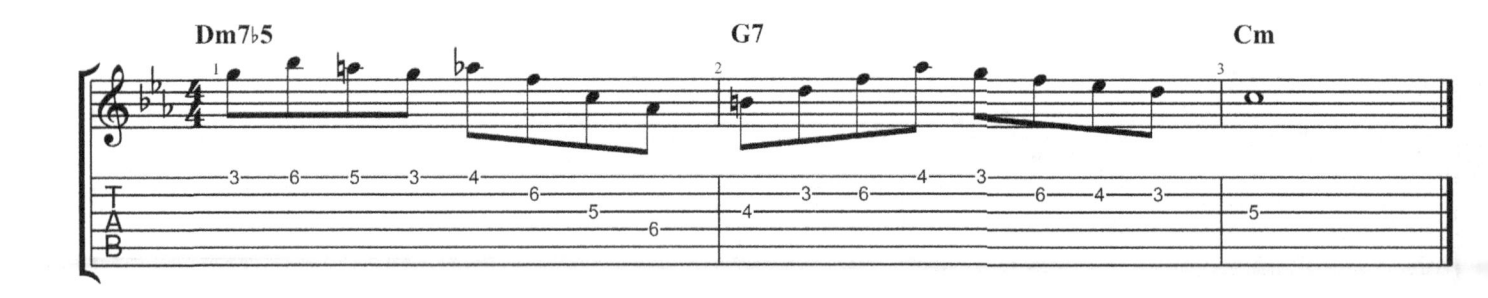

Example 3z14

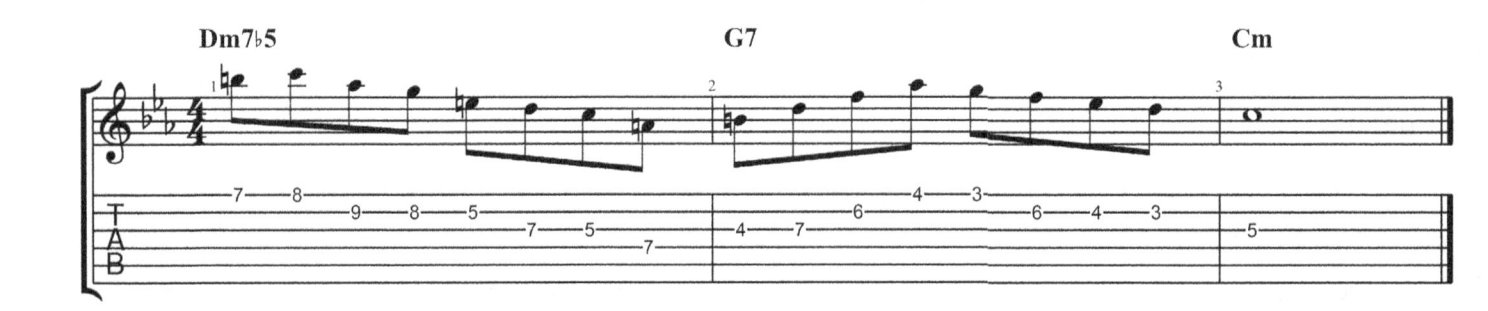

Here are two lines that use Cell 3.

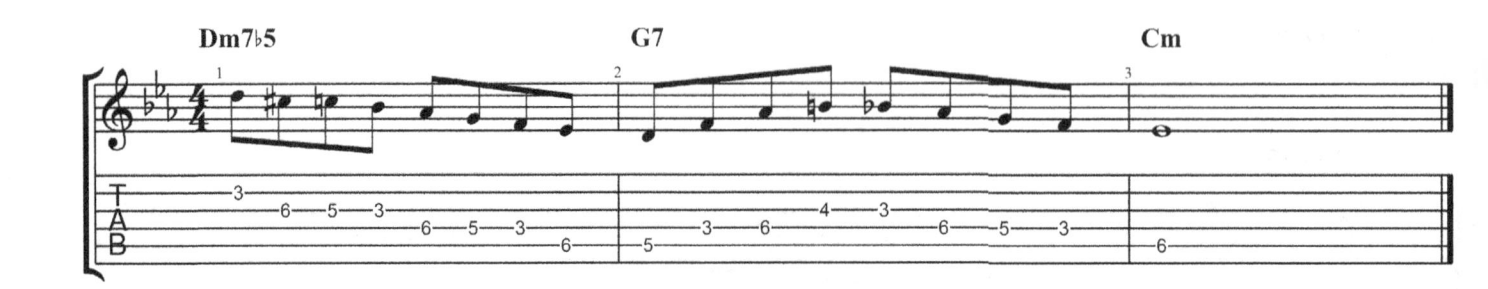

Example 3z15

Example 3z16

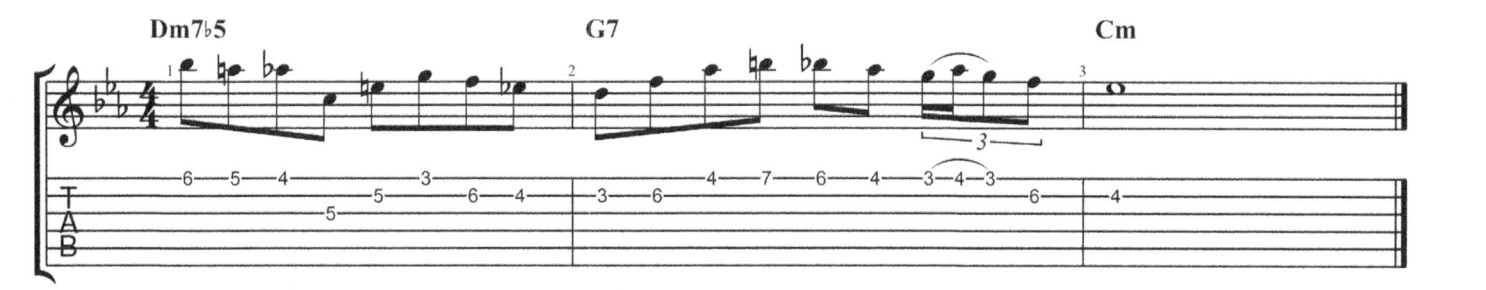

And two lines for Cell 4.

Example 3z17

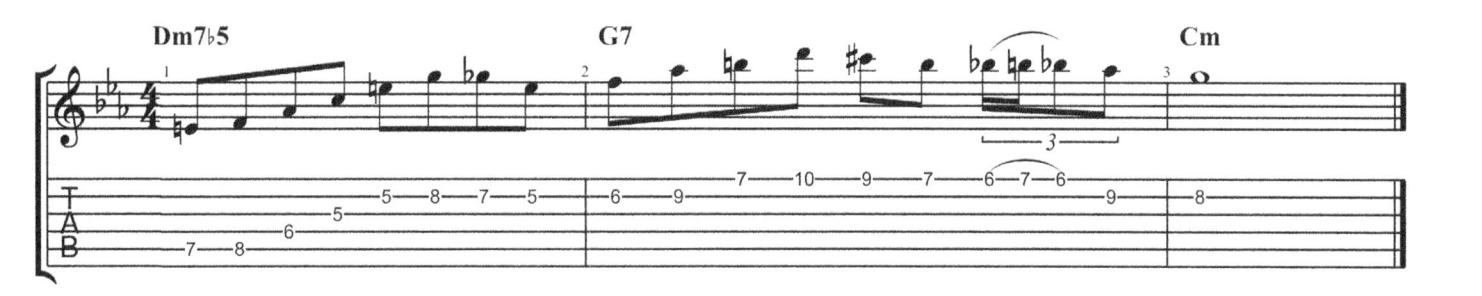

Example 3z18

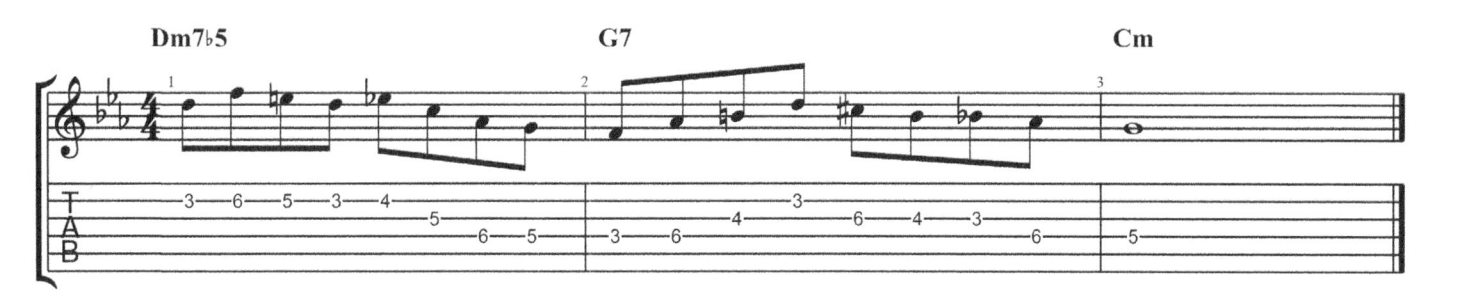

More advanced cellular vocabulary

As before, now we can add some different phrasing ideas to turn these cellular ideas into useable licks. Remember, whenever you encounter a line that you particularly like, be sure to memorize it, then transpose it into other keys and test it out over a favorite jazz standard.

First, five lines that use Cell 1 from the b9 (Ab).

This first line uses the diminished scale in bar one with an added chromatic passing note. Triplets help to change up the cell.

Example 3z19

The phrase in bar one of the next example is an arpeggio lick. It plays with the underlying harmony a little as collectively the notes suggest the sound of Dm11.

Example 3z20

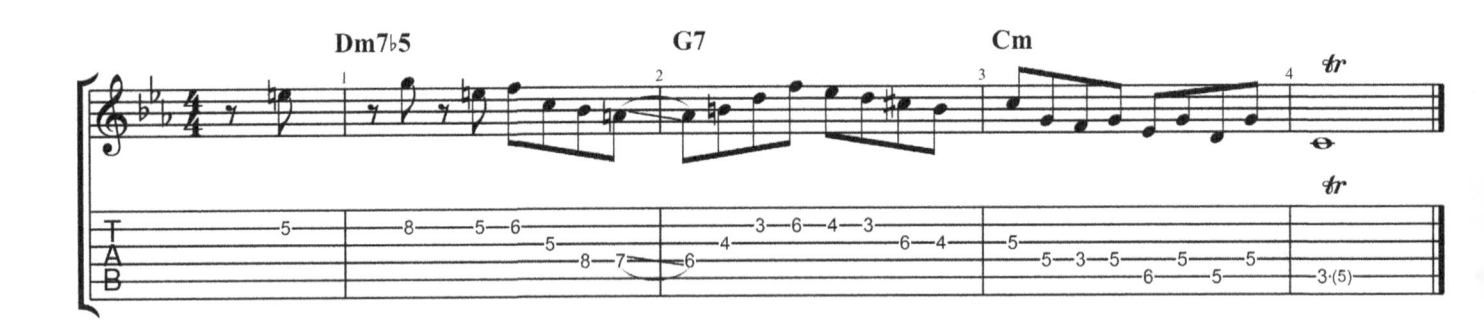

We're back to the diminished scale in bar one of this line, and the cell is bar two is simply displaced to begin on the 1& of the bar.

Example 3z21

Here's a useful arpeggio lick you can play over the change from Dm7b5 to G7. It uses the chord tones of Dm7b5 but adds in the 9th, and the phrase ends on an outside sounding A note that provides a half step resolution to the Ab of the cell in bar two.

Example 3z22

The next idea uses the straight C Natural Minor scale in bar one, but again adds in the outside A note to resolve to the cell.

Example 3z23

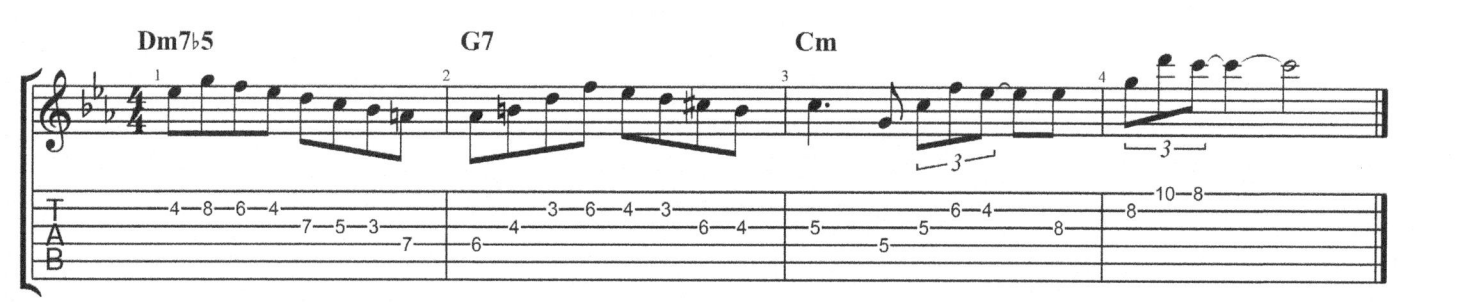

Now we move on to five lines that use Cell 2, from the 3rd (B).

The lick in bar one here is a staple bebop idea that is often played over minor quality chords. Here it's adapted into the diminished scale where it takes on a much more interesting color.

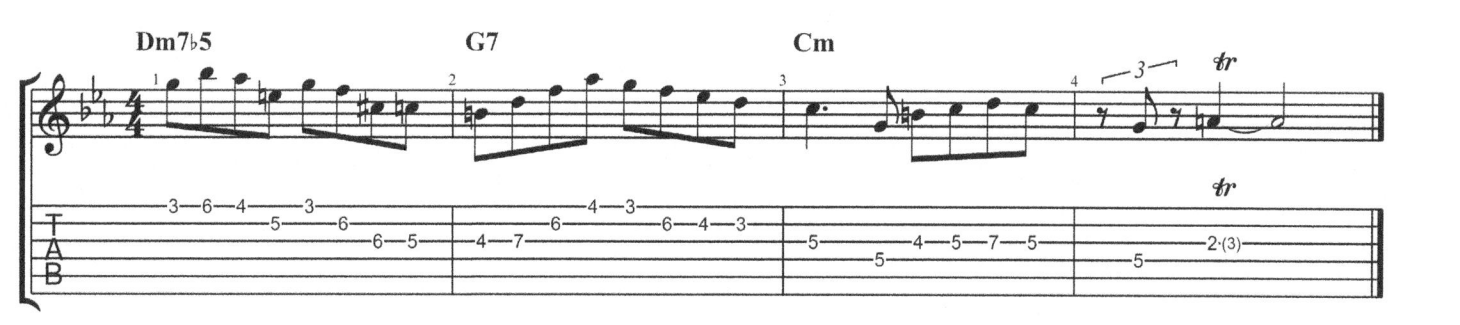

Example 3z24

The diminished scale is great for producing dark-sounding moody lines like this one. The scale's #11 interval is instrumental in achieving this. The effect of this interval over the ii chord is to imply a complex Dm(Maj7)#11 tonality.

Example 3z25

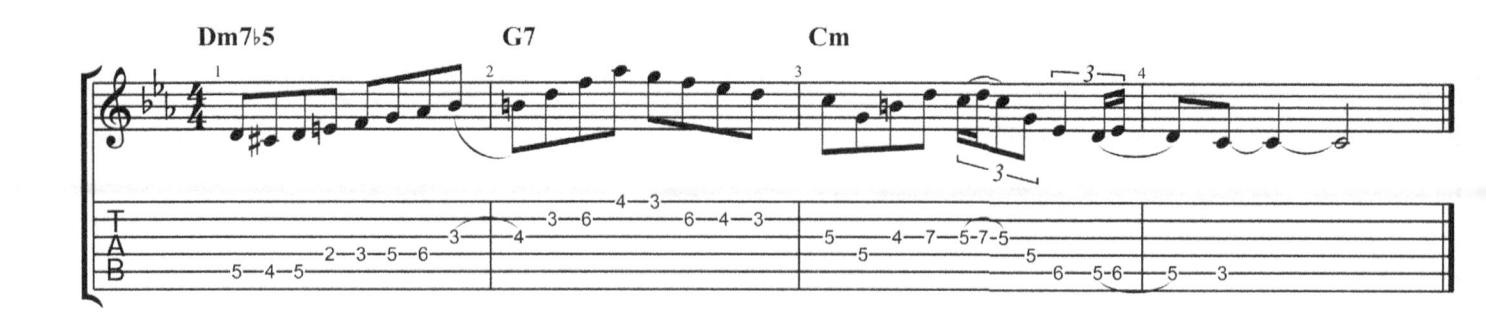

Next, here's an idea to help you break away from linear thinking, with some string-skipped intervals. Again, the C# note plays a leading role in making the line sound tense and angular. The phrasing of bar one is mimicked in bar two.

Example 3z26

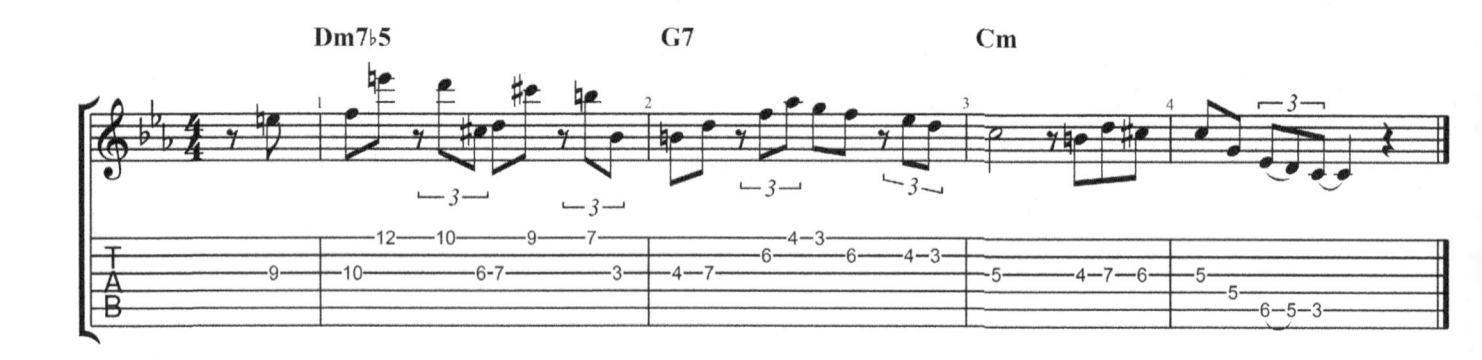

This line begins with another standard bebop idea using the C Natural Minor scale but it is tweaked to include an E (the 9th over Dm7b5) rather than Eb.

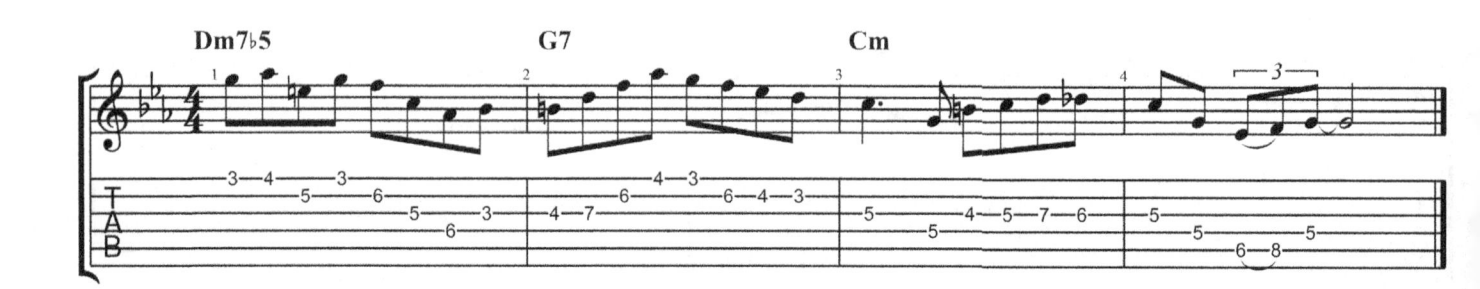

Example 3z27

Here's an idea that mixes up G Half-Whole Diminished intervals in bar one to create an ascending pattern that dovetails nicely with the cell in bar two.

Example 3z28

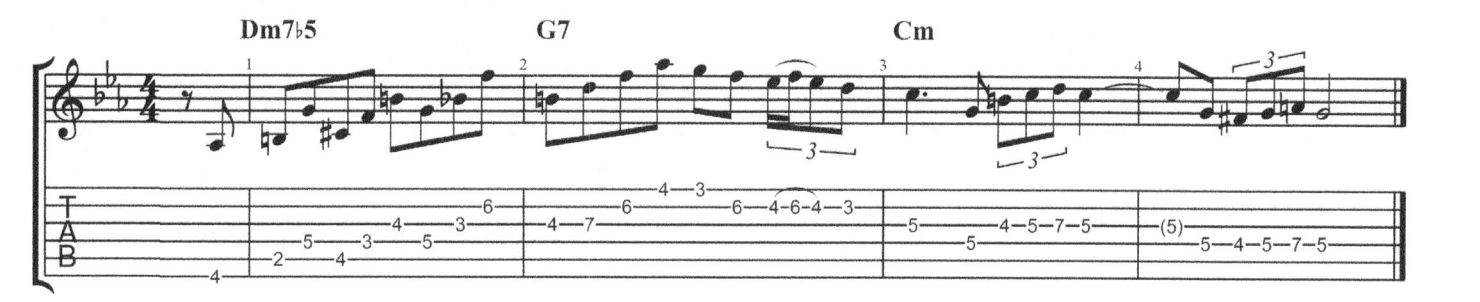

Now let's explore five lines that use Cell 3 from the 5th (D) of G7.

The phrase in bar one here is a similar idea to the previous example, only in descending form. In a way, it's a Coltrane type approach to melody creation, where arpeggio or scale tones are sequenced into four-note patterns and played in a "cascading" manner, either ascending or descending. It's an idea that players like Michael Brecker took and spent years developing to new heights. Both musicians thought in a cellular way.

Example 3z29

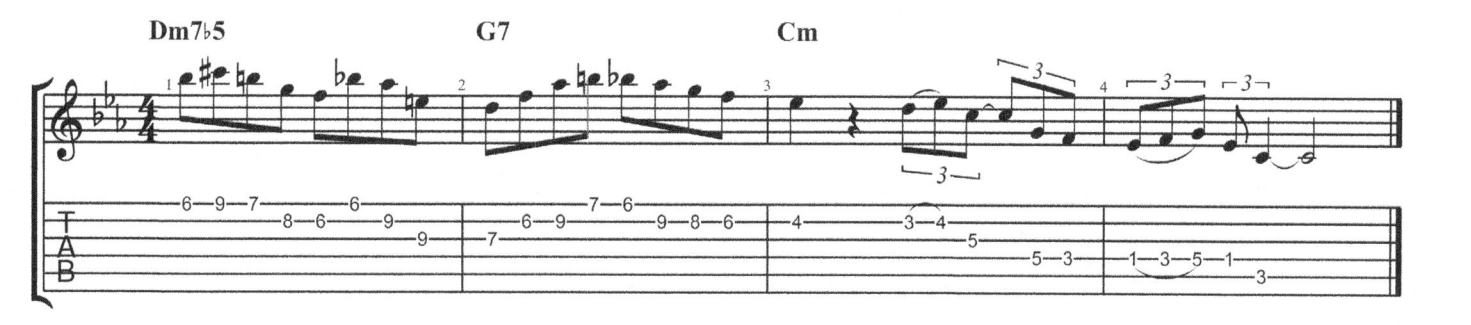

Examples 3z30 through 3z32 all exemplify this Coltrane/Brecker approach. The first two examples use the diminished scale in bar one and Example 3z32 achieves the same with a hybrid line – the first four-note phrase coming from the diminished and the next from C Natural Minor.

Example 3z30

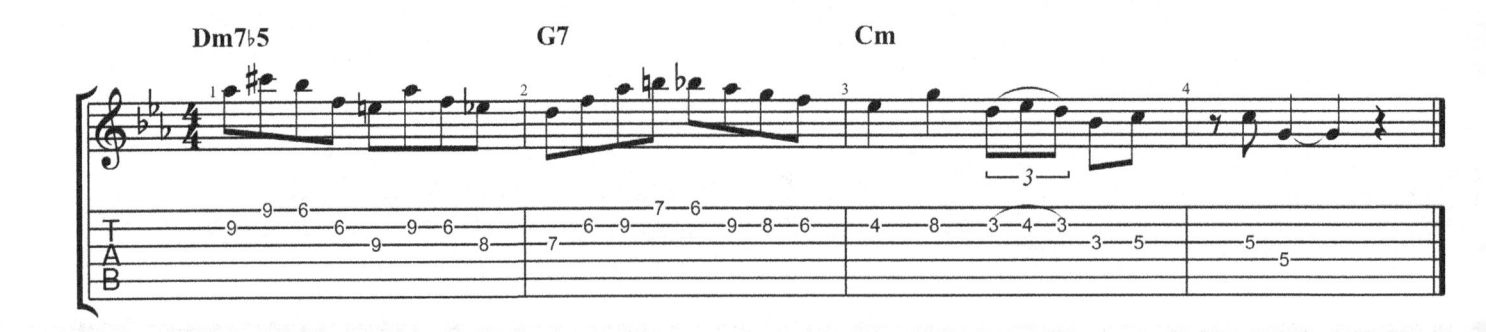

Example 3z31

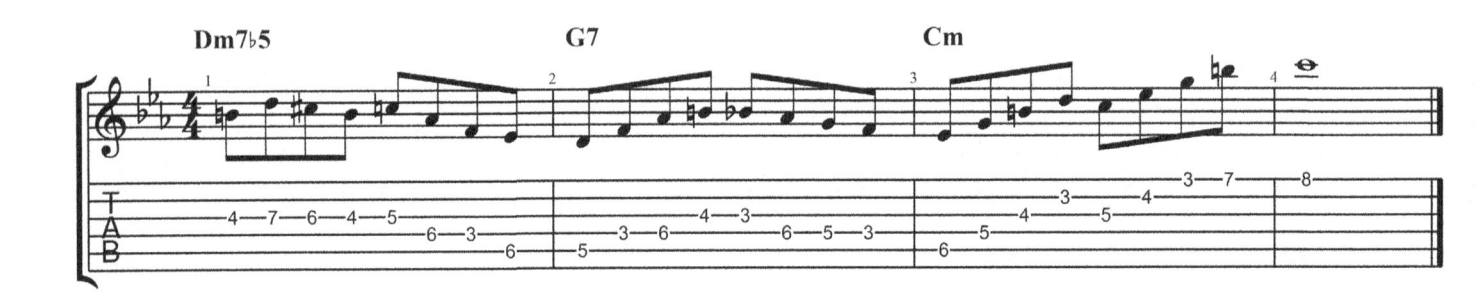

Example 3z32

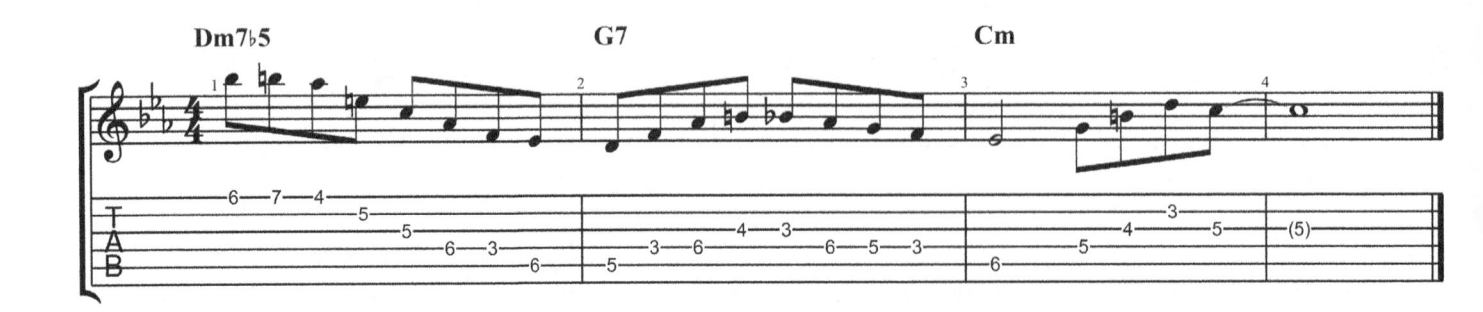

In the example below, the phrasing is arranged so that the four-note phrases cross the bar line. This really helps to disguise the cell in bar two because it's part of a phrase that clearly begins in the previous bar, and the same thing happens at the end of bar two.

Example 3z33

Lastly, here are five melodic lines that use Cell 4 from the b7 (F) of G7.

The first line uses the diminished scale in bar one but has a couple of passing notes added in which disguise it. Listen carefully to the audio to nail the articulations in this phrase.

Example 3z34

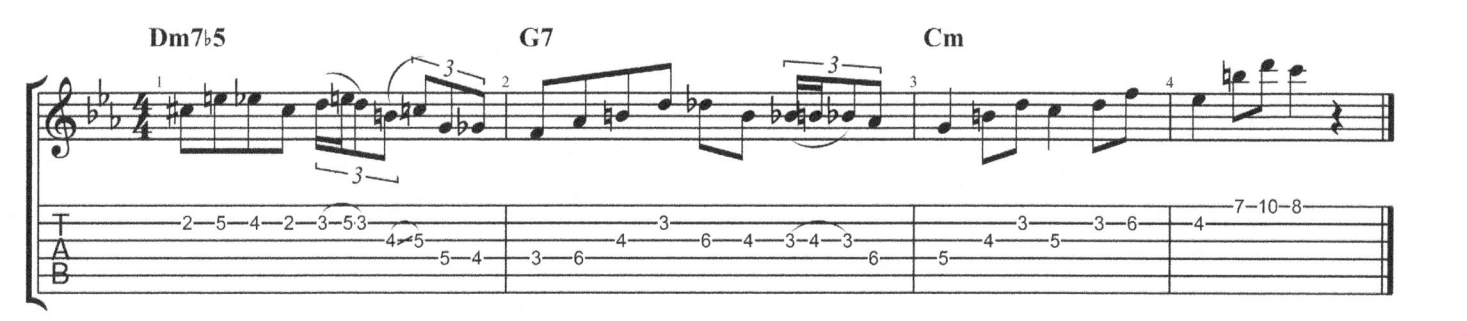

Here's another angular sounding sequenced idea to lead into the cell. The phrase in bar one is built entirely from 5th intervals using G Half-Whole Diminished.

Example 3z35

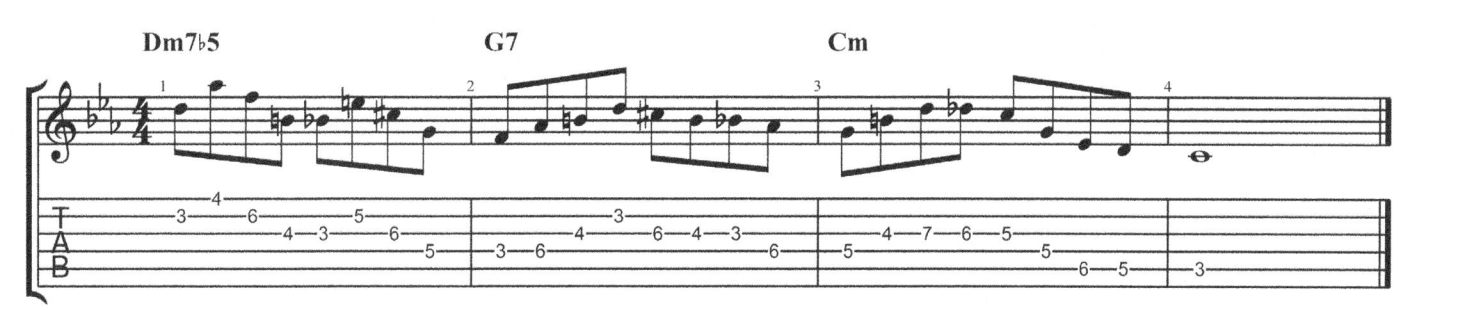

The next line uses a similar idea. This time the phrase in bar one alternates between 4th and 6th intervals. (There are extensive exercises to master the diminished scale intervallically in my book *Inside-Outside Guitar Soloing* by Fundamental Changes if you want to check that out).

Example 3z36

Here's a useful opening lick that ascends the C Natural Minor scale. It ends on an E rather than Eb to make a half step resolution to the F note of the cell in bar two.

Example 3z37

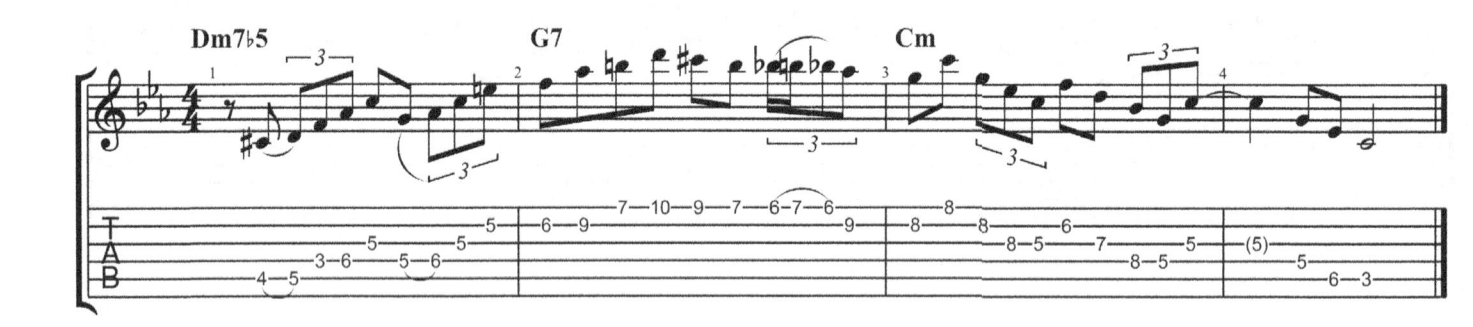

To end our exploration of the diminished scale over the minor ii V i, here is another intervallic lick with some string skips. The notes in bar one are organized into 3rds.

Example 3z38

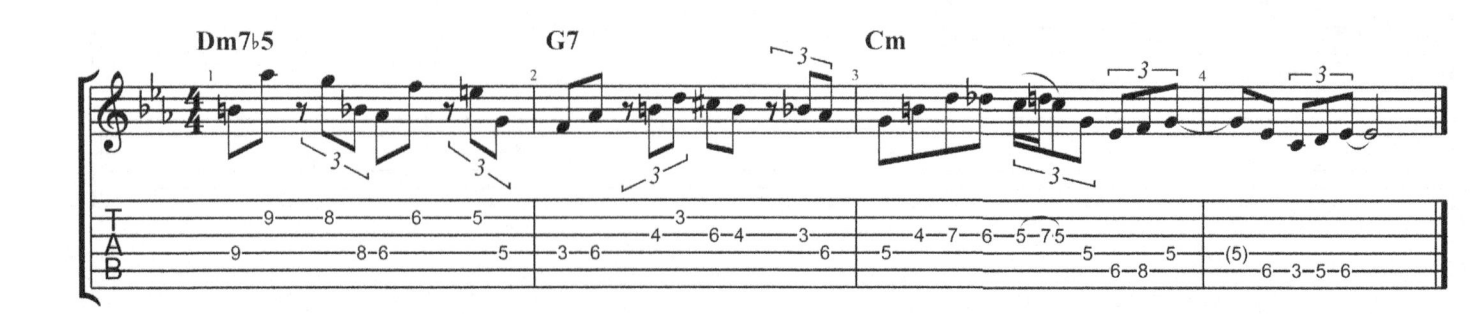

Chapter Four – Altered Scale Cells

The Altered scale originates from the Melodic Minor scale. Also known as the Super Locrian, it is the seventh mode of the Melodic Minor and contains all the altered tensions that can be added to a dominant chord. An easy way to think about this scale is to see it as a Mixolydian scale where all the non-defining chords tones have been altered by being both sharpened *and* flattened.

Take a look at the notes/intervals of G Mixolydian, then compare them to G Altered below.

G Mixolydian:

G	A	B	C	D	E	F
Root	9th	3rd	11th	5th	13th	b7

Compared to G Mixolydian, the G Altered scale has the 5th and 9th intervals both flattened and sharpened. G Altered no longer has the natural 5th (D) of a G7 chord, but the root, 3rd and b7 chord tones remain the same (the root, 3rd and 7th can't be altered without changing the quality of the chord, but every other note can be altered by raising it or lowering it a half step).

G Altered:

G	Ab	Bb	B	Db	Eb	F
Root	b9	#9	3rd	b5	#5	b7

The altered tensions make this scale a perfect choice for easy access to some vivid color tensions over dominant chords. We can choose to target specific tension notes within the scale, such as just the b9 sound, or we can use all the available tensions to create more complex inside-outside melodic lines. When it comes to creating our melodic cells, you'll see that they contain different combinations of these tensions.

Scale shapes

In terms of its layout on the fretboard, I've always viewed the Altered scale as a combination of the Diminished and Whole Tone scales and understanding this makes it much easier to learn. Here is how I visualize it on the fretboard. Take a look at this third position scale shape:

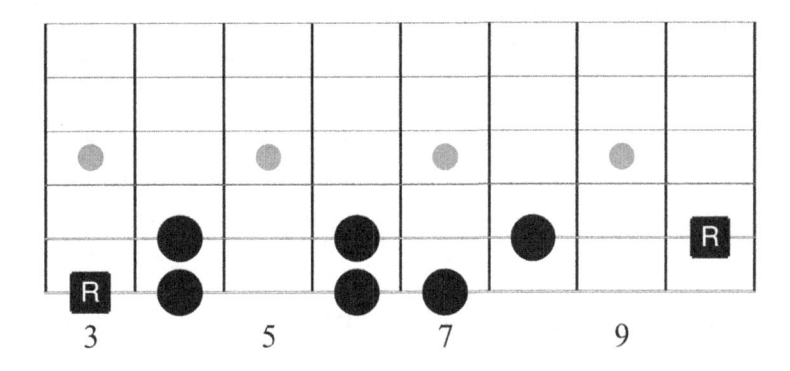

Notice that the four notes on the sixth string mirror the intervals of the Diminished scale, while the four notes on the fifth string mirror the pattern of the Whole Tone scale.

We can use the G root note to connect these scale fragments together and create a crawling pattern which repeats. This is my preferred pattern to ascend/descend the neck rapidly, covering a wide range of the fretboard.

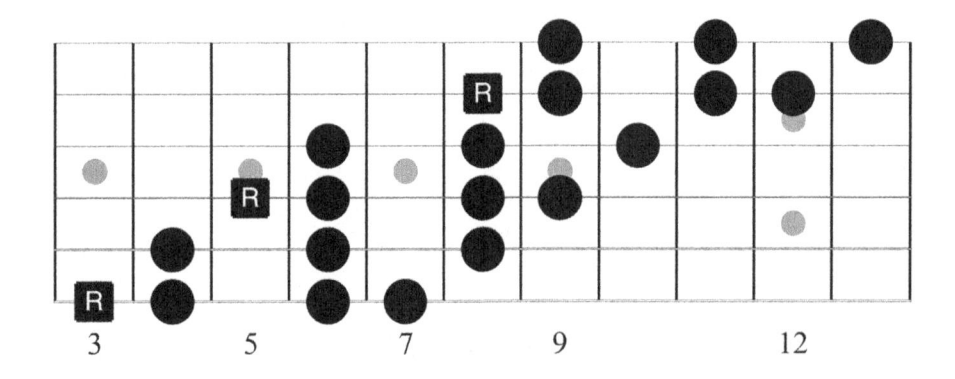

If you find it a stretch to play four notes on one string, especially in the lower register, then add in a position slide, just like we did for the diminished scale.

The melodic cells

Now let's look at the four melodic cells we can create using the G Altered scale.

First, from the G root note. Notice that Cell 1 contains both #5 (Eb) and b5 (Db) tension notes.

Example 4a – Cell 1

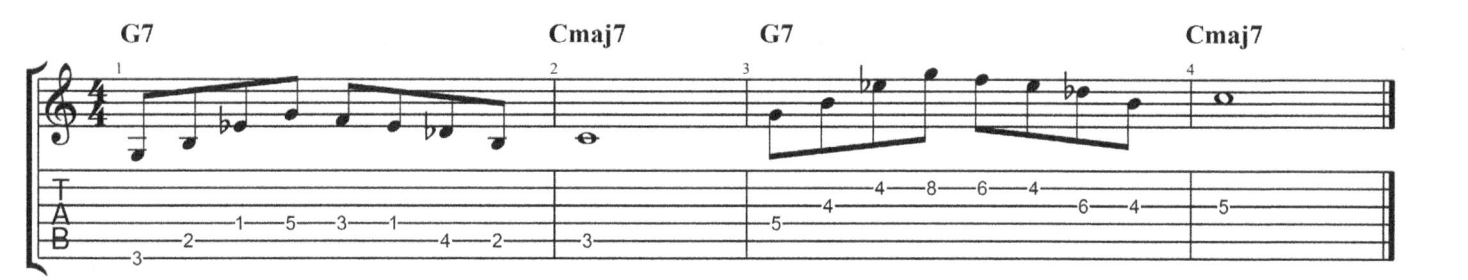

Next, here is the cell built from the 3rd (B) of G7. This cell has #5, #9 and b9 tensions.

Example 4b – Cell 2

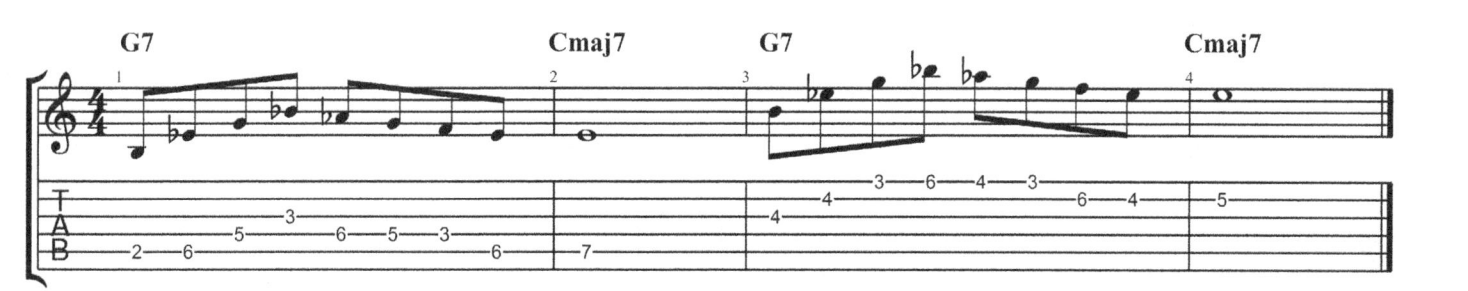

The G Altered scale doesn't contain a D note, so when we come to Cell 3, we once again begin it from the #5 (Eb). Notice that this cell contains (in order) the #5, #9, b5 and b9 – every note that can be altered on a G7 chord without changing its quality.

Example 4c – Cell 3

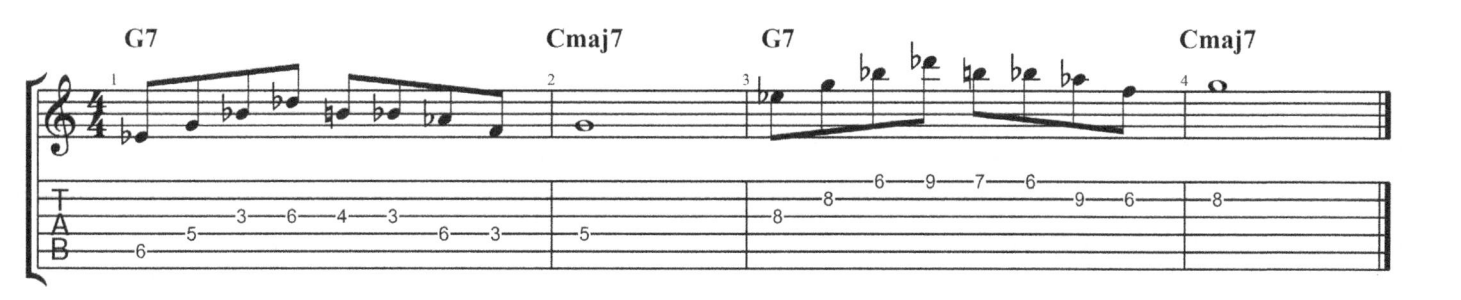

And lastly, Cell 4 built from the b7 (F) of G7. This cell also contains all four altered tension notes.

Example 4d – Cell 4

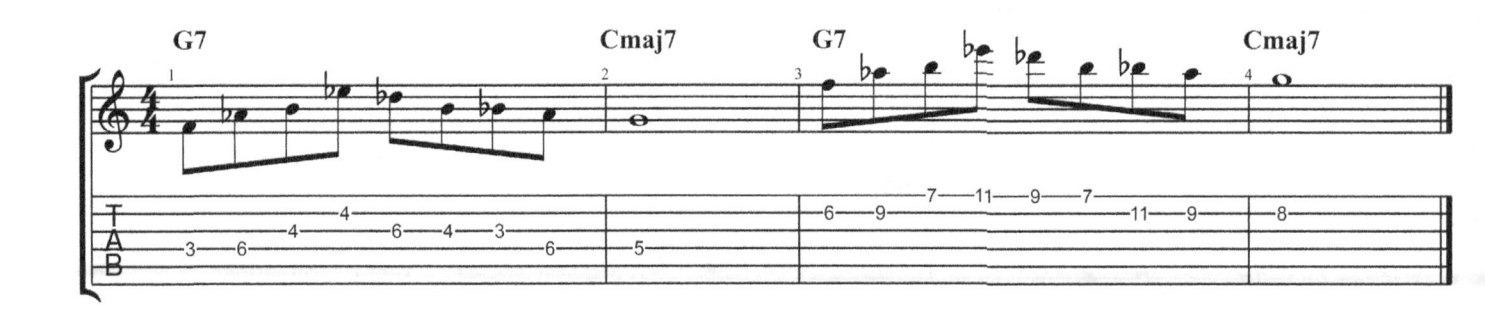

Putting the cells into a Major ii V I

The altered scale has a very different sound to the Mixolydian, Whole Tone and Diminished scales we've explored in previous chapters. As its scale pattern on the fretboard suggests, it's like the first four notes of the Diminished scale fused together with the last three notes of the Whole Tone scale. It's this hybrid nature that makes it so useful for creating interesting melodic lines.

As before, we'll get accustomed to its sound by playing two simple lines for each cell. First, two lines using Cell 1 from the G root note.

Example 4e

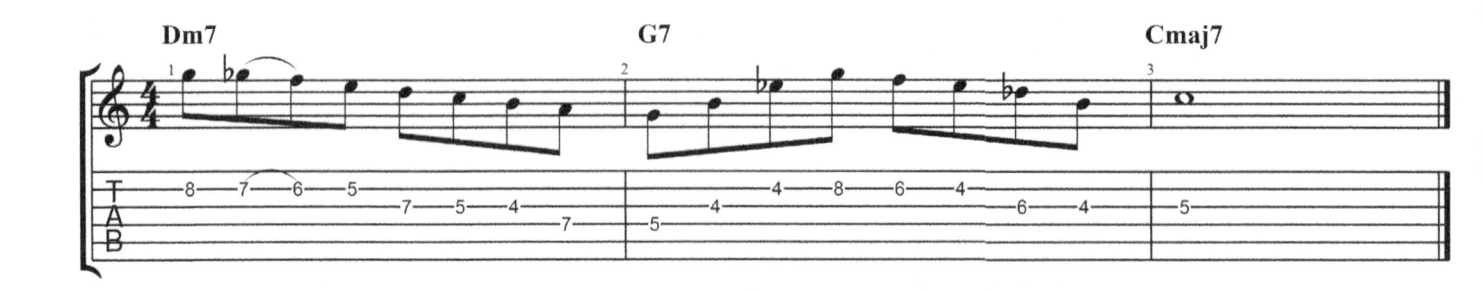

Example 4f

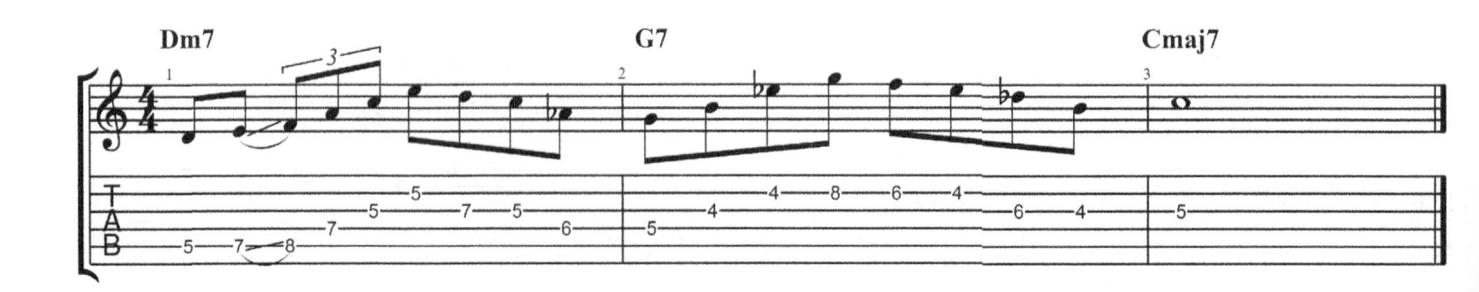

Next, two lines for Cell 2, from 3rd (B).

Example 4g

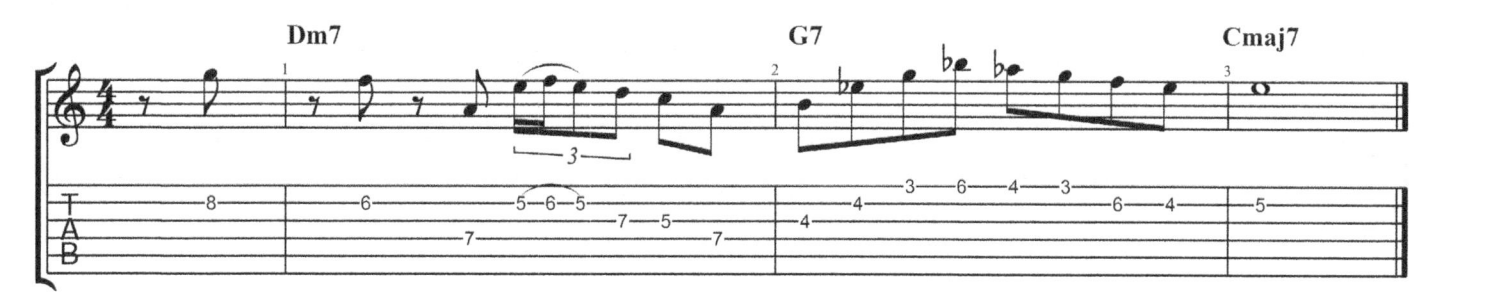

Example 4h

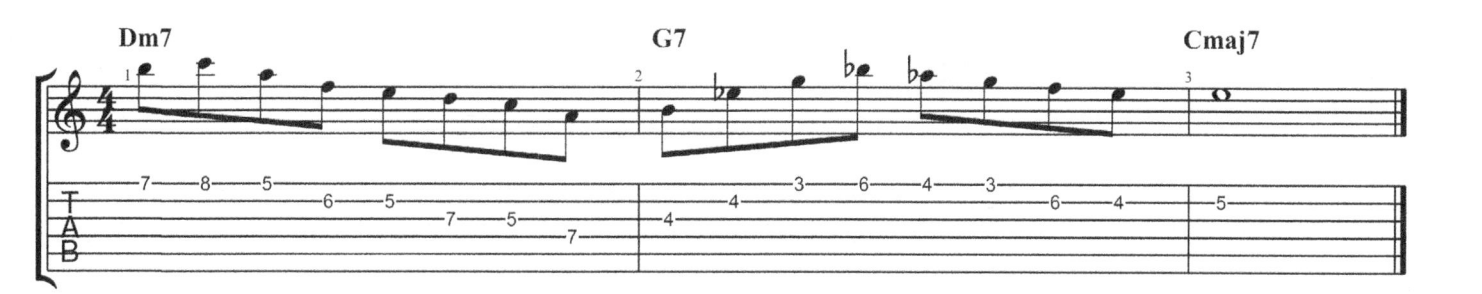

Next, here are two Cell 3 lines, launching from the #5 interval (Eb) of the scale.

Example 4i

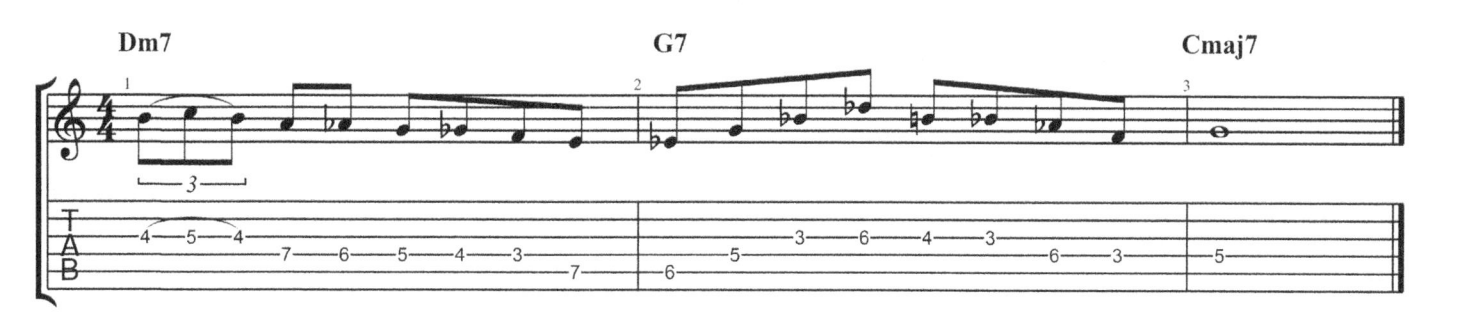

Example 4j

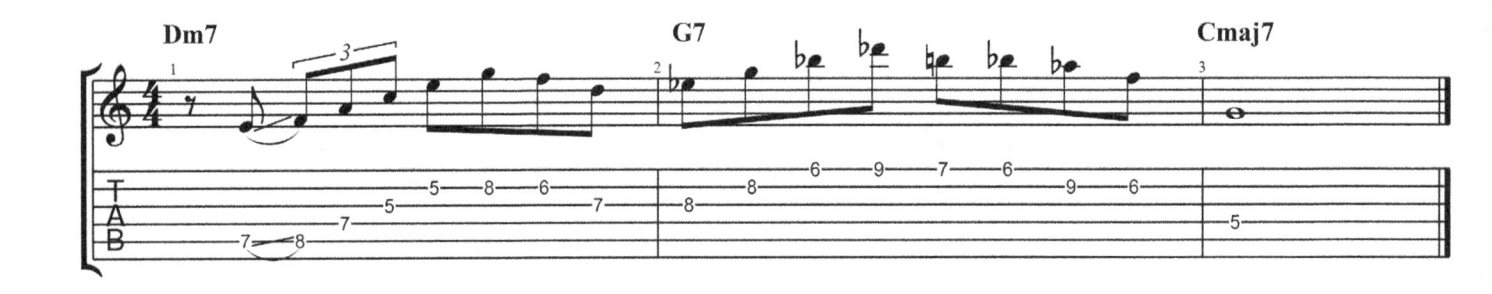

And lastly, two simple lines for Cell 4 from the b7 (F).

Example 4k

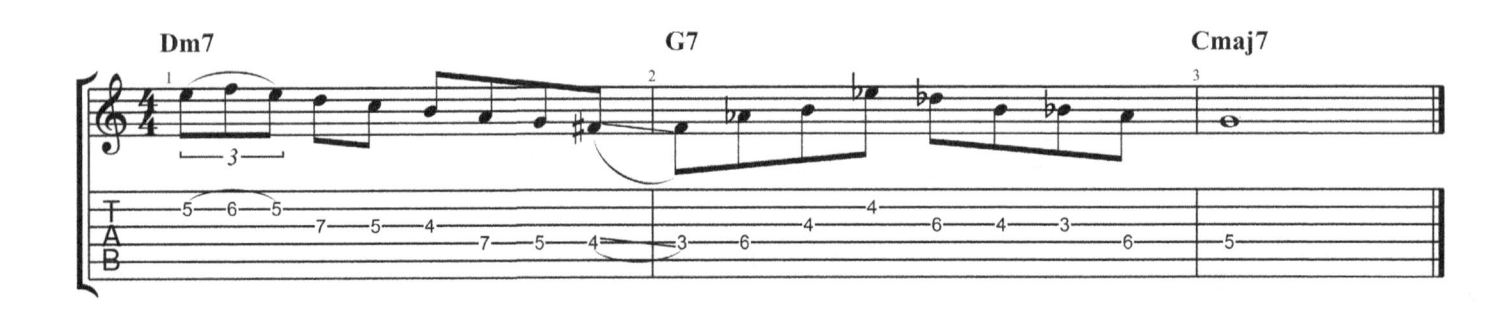

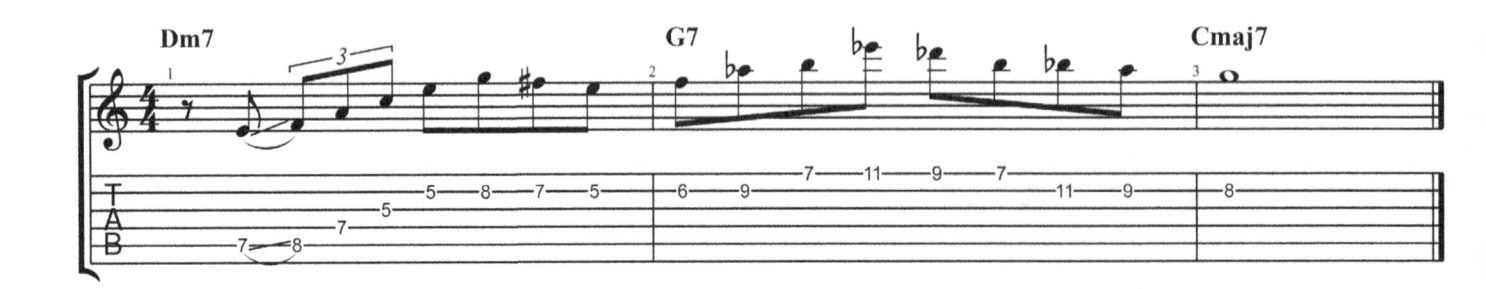

Example 4l

More advanced cellular vocabulary

Now it's time to use our altered cell vocabulary in the context of a set of Major ii V I lines.

This first idea uses some chromatic passing notes in bar one, so that the first note of Cell 1 is targeted with a passing note from above. Another half step resolution gets us to the root of Cmaj7 in bar three.

Example 4m

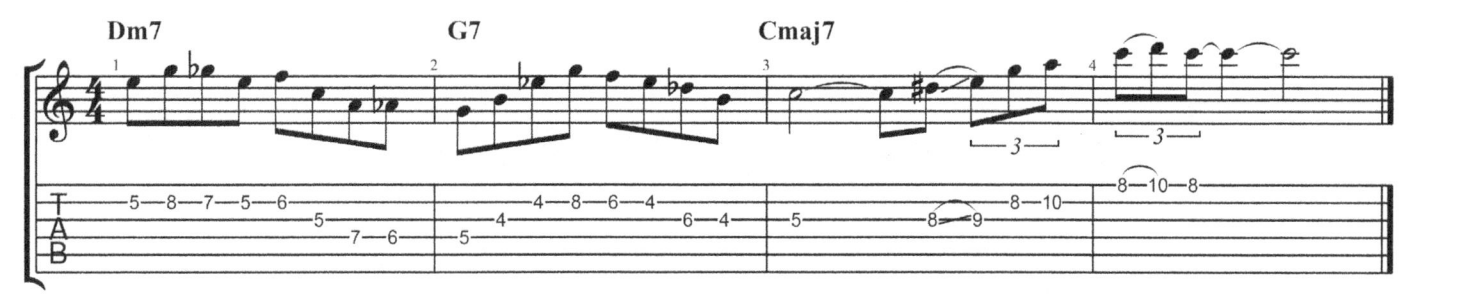

This line uses the G Altered scale in bar one. Over a Dm7 chord, the scale's tension notes represent the major 7th, b9 and b5.

Example 4n

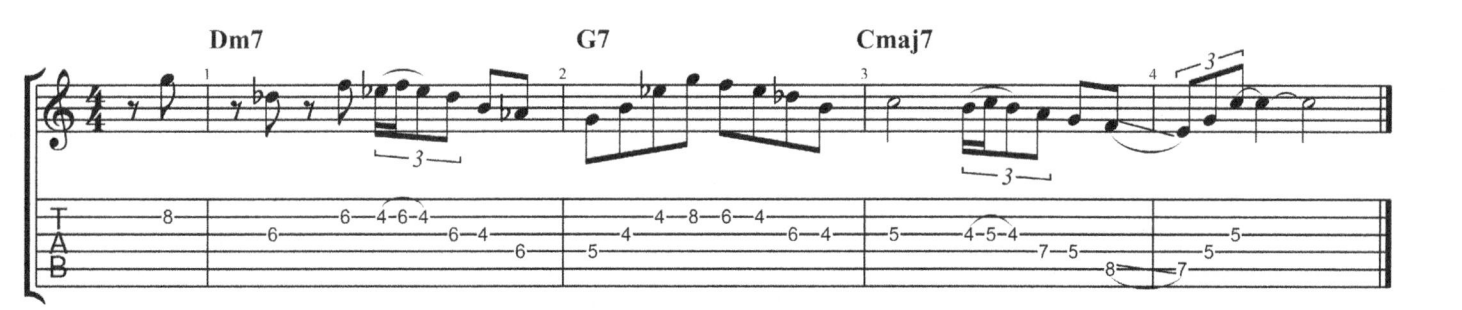

Example 4o uses just the C Major scale either side of the cell, with one passing note in bar three. The cell in bar two is altered rhythmically.

Example 4o

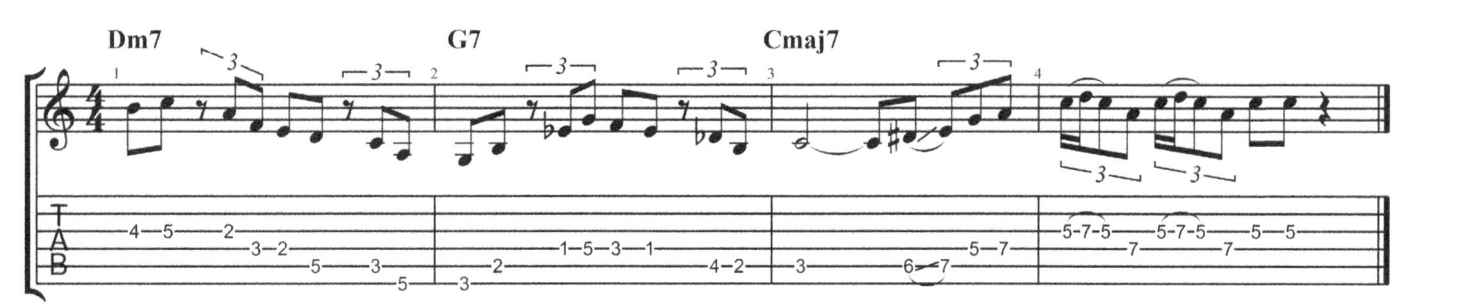

In Example 4p, the line begins with an enclosure type idea. In bar one, the first four-note phrase is targeting the F chord tone (the 3rd of Dm7) that falls on beat 3. From here the G Altered scale takes over for the second four-note phrase, which resolves a half step to the cell in bar two. Take care to capture the timing of the ascending run in bars 3-4.

Example 4p

Here's another string-skipping intervallic idea to mix things up. In bar one the intervals are alternating 3rds and 6ths.

Example 4q

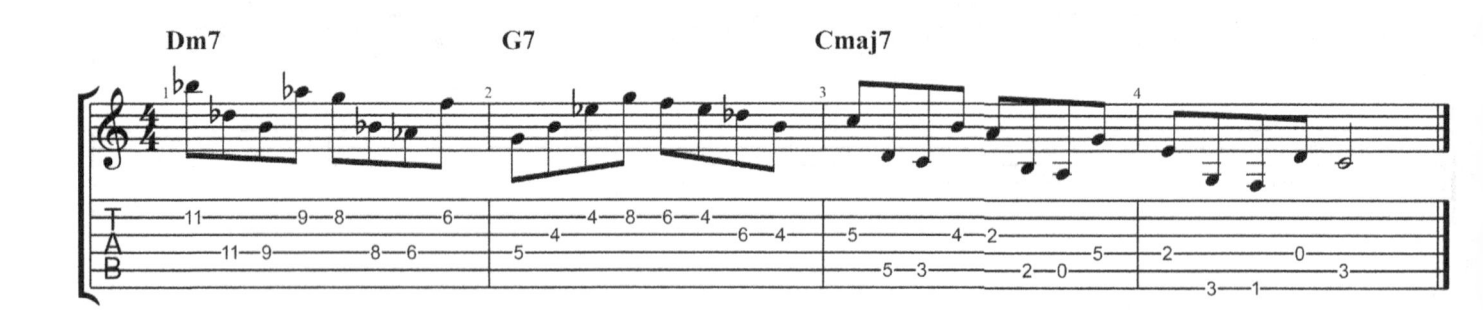

Now let's look at five lines that use Cell 2 from the 3rd (B).

A straight C Major ascending run in bar one ends with a Bb passing note to resolve to the B of the cell.

Example 4r

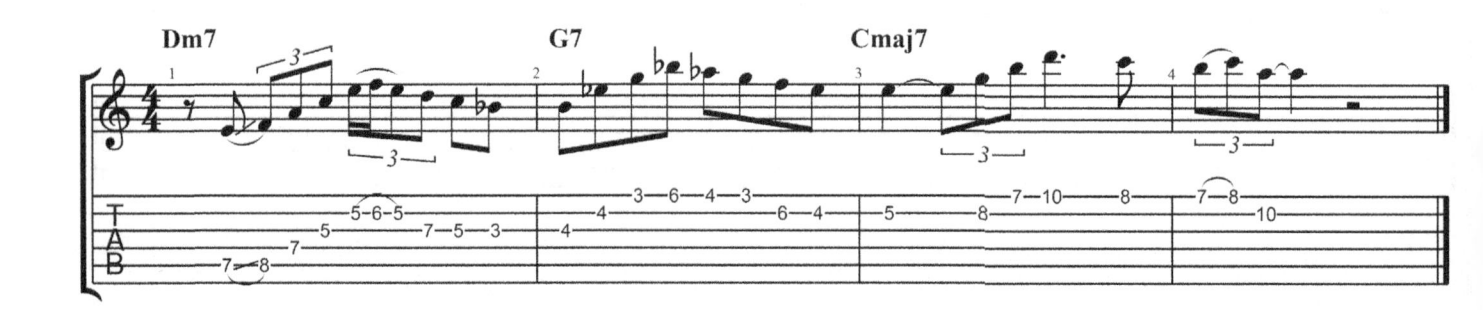

In the next line, the opening phrase uses some 4th intervals with the C Major scale to avoid playing a stepwise movement. The phrasing idea continues in bars 3-4.

Example 4s

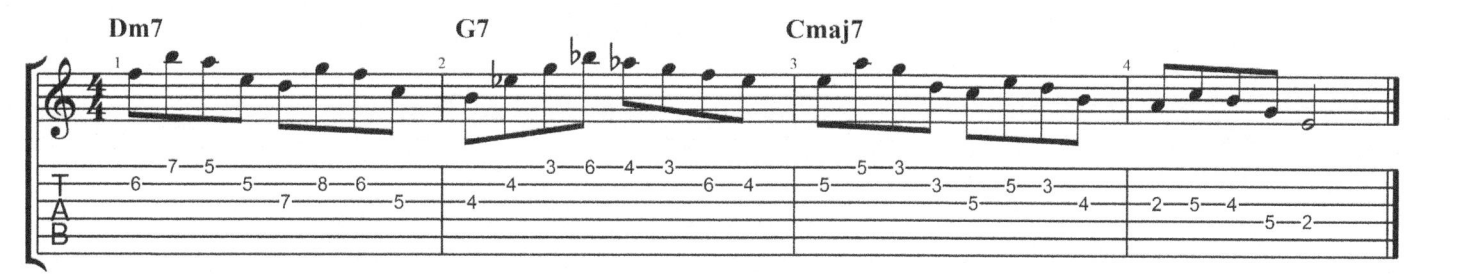

In the next line, the G Altered scale is used to create the phrase in bar one, but with the addition of the C "home" note of the key. It's a simple idea that makes it easier for our ears to accept all the altered tensions that are happening.

Example 4t

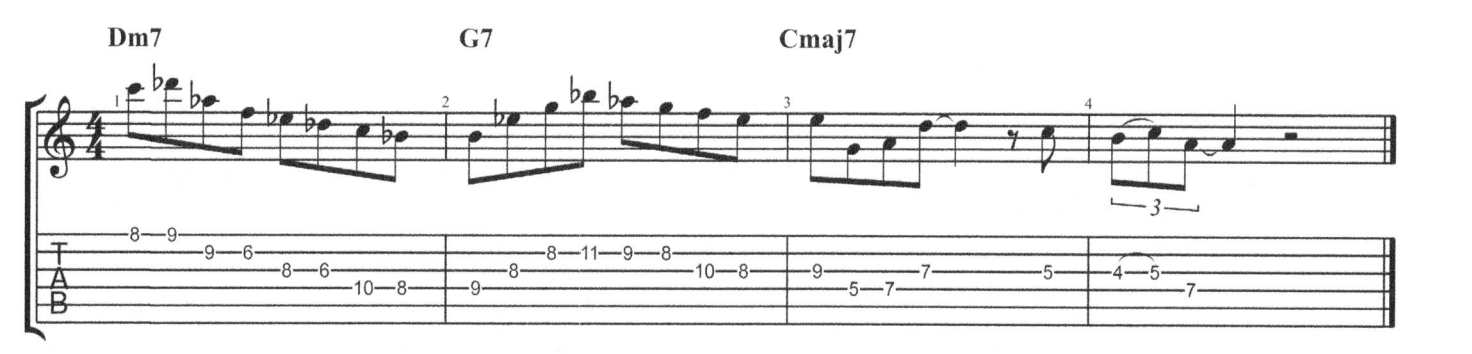

The idea that opens the next line is pure bebop phrasing but, of course, adapted for the altered scale, which enables it to take on a new flavor.

Example 4u

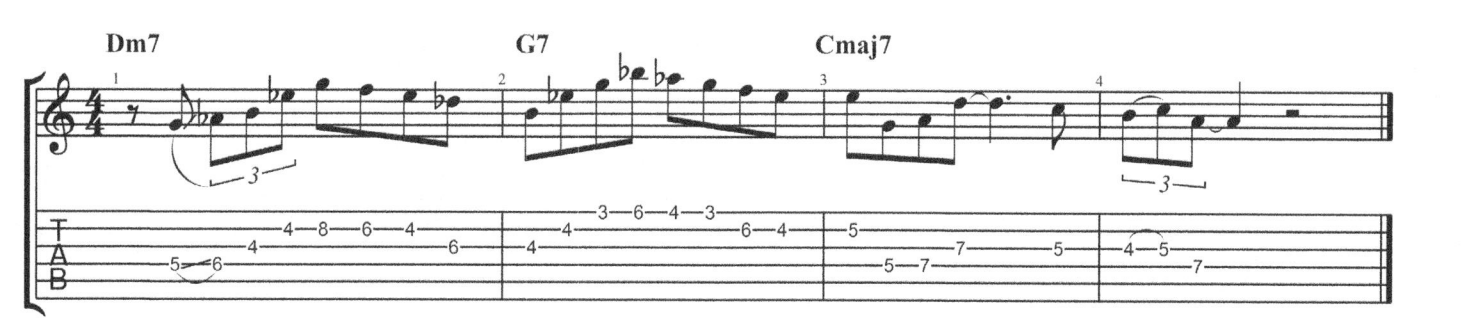

Next we have a C Major scale line but with a couple of passing notes. The aim in bar one is to target the B note of the cell chromatically from above.

Example 4v

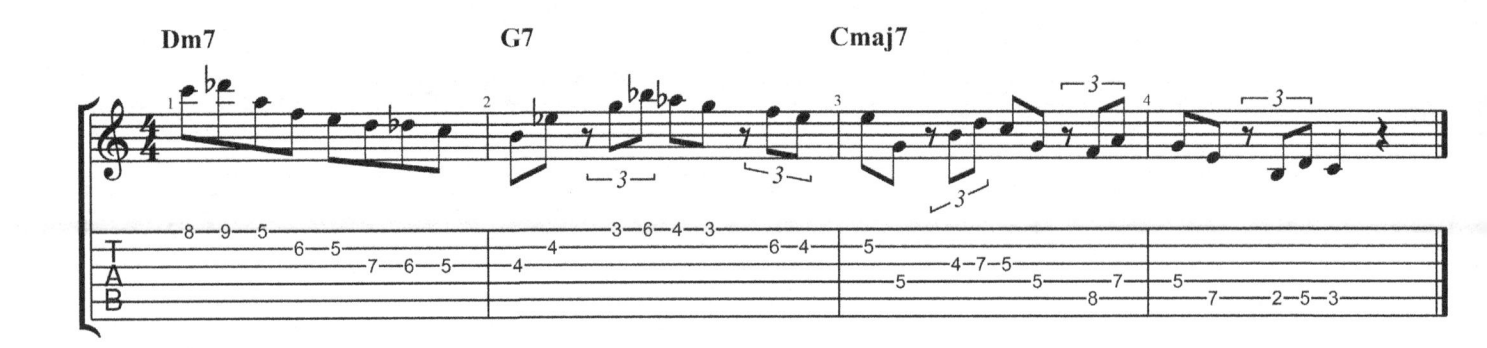

Let's move on with the collection of lines built using Cell 3, from the #5 interval.

Bar one of the first example uses standard bebop vocabulary to play an enclosure around the C root note. The E scale note at the end of bar one resolves nicely to the Eb that launches the cell.

Example 4w

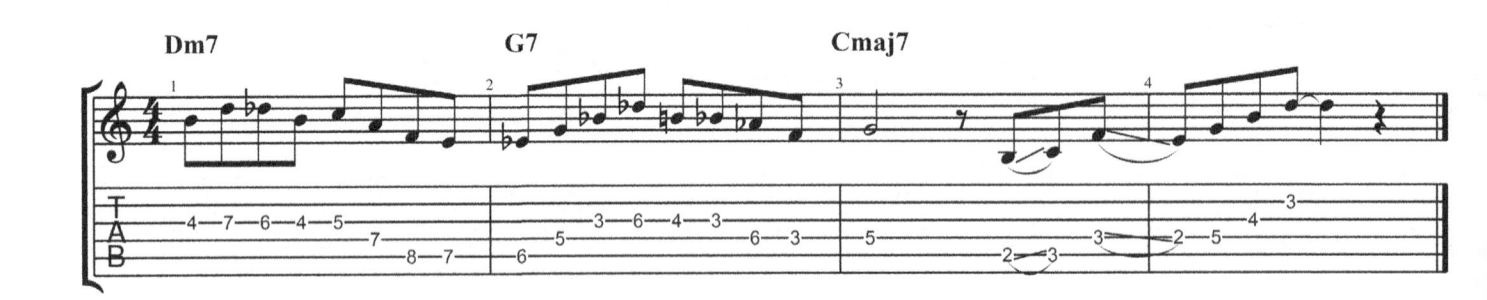

This line uses a chromatic descent to resolve to the higher register expression of the cell.

Example 4x

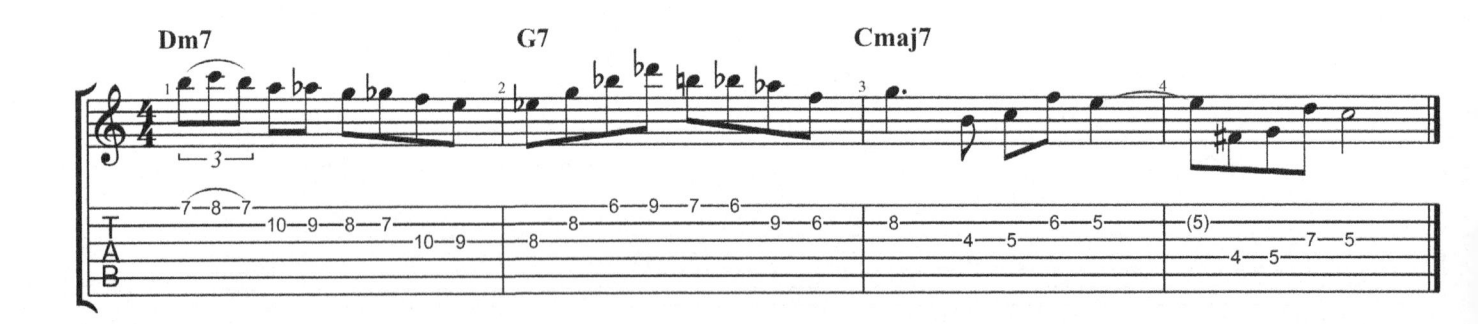

The next example begins with a pedal tone idea, pivoting on the B note. Bars 3-4 have another common bop lick to close out the line.

Example 4y

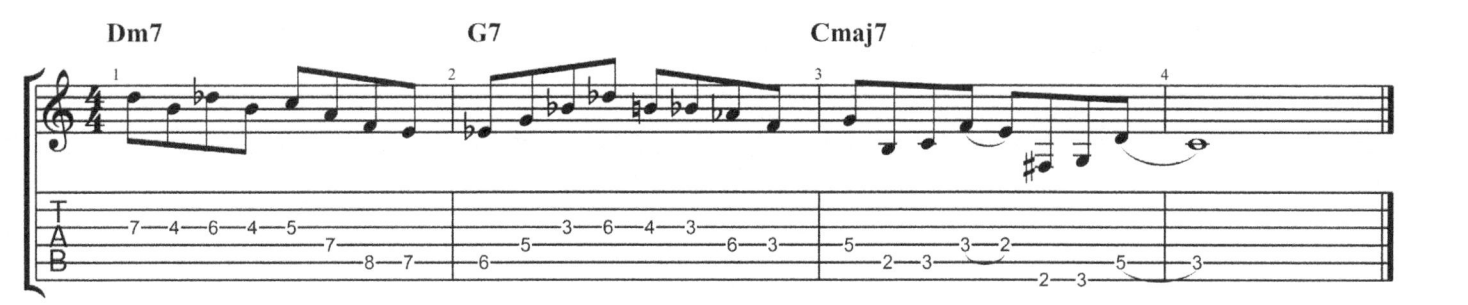

In Example 4z the altered scale is played over the Dm7 chord, but several of the scale tones are preceded by a chromatic note from below to create a sequence. The phrasing of this sequence is picked up again in bars 3-4. We need to add one passing note (F#) to retain the shape of the phrase.

Example 4z

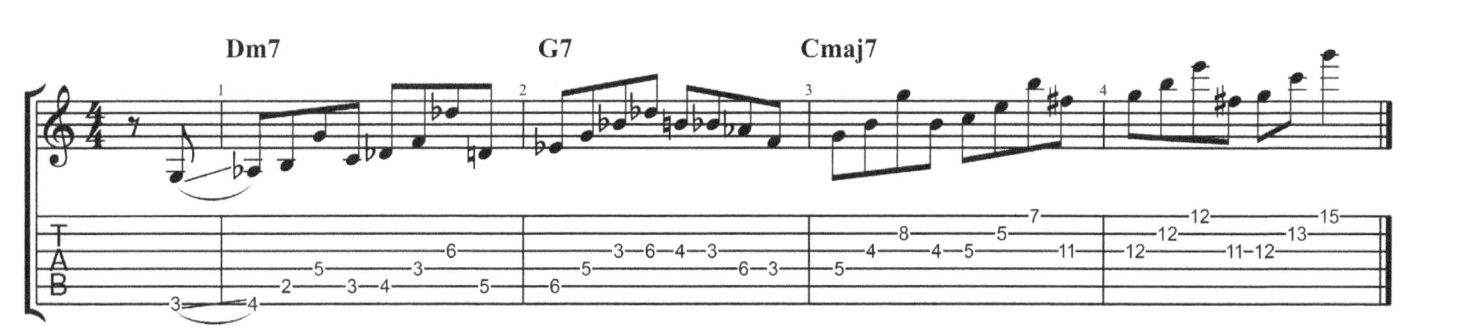

In the next example, the cellular phrase is displaced by an 1/8th note then broken up rhythmically so that it crosses the bar line into bar three.

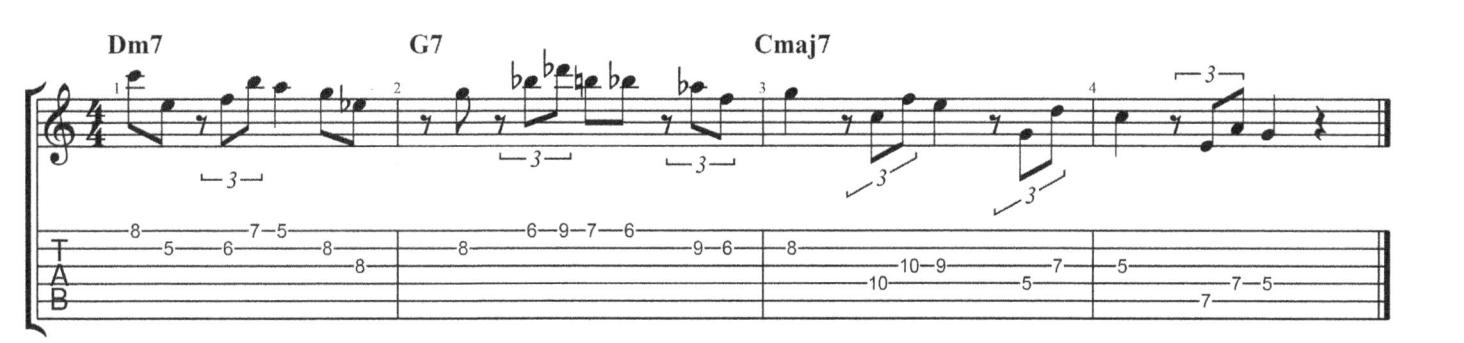

Example 4z1

To finish this Major ii V I section, here are five ways of using Cell 4, from the b7 (F) of G7.

To kick things off, here's another line that uses 1/8th note triplet rests at regular intervals to break up the phrasing.

Example 4z2

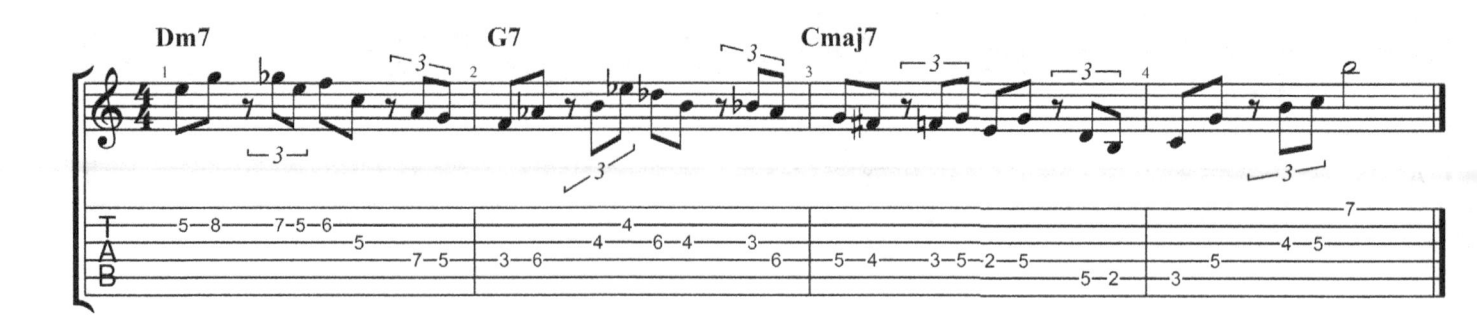

Example 4z3 uses an idea in bar one that we saw near the beginning of this book. There are some notes that belong to the G Altered scale here and others that don't, but in fact the idea is quite simple: it's a side stepping movement where, instead of playing a D minor line, we're playing Eb minor – a half step above. The phrase is based around a 2nd position inversion of Ebm.

Whenever we transpose a lick chromatically, by a half step up or down, it invariably produces a set of tension tones that result in an outside sounding line. Often, these will be altered notes, but they may also be extended notes and the results can be surprising.

The three main tension notes at work in bar one are Gb, Eb and Bb. In order they represent #9, b9 and b13 intervals over Dm7. If you've never thought to try something like this, experiment in your next practice session and analyze the results!

Example 4z3

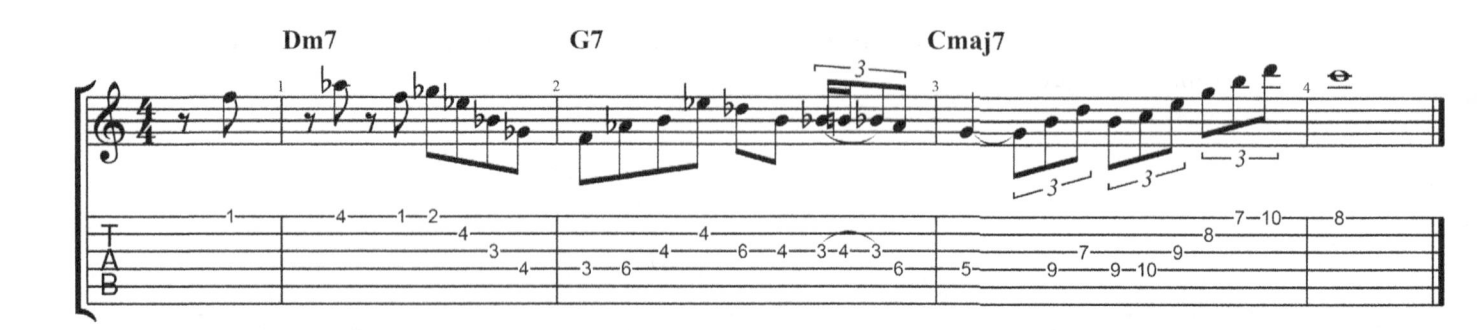

After a straight run down the C Major scale, a passing note leads into the cell in this line. Notice the use of passing notes over the Cmaj7 chord too.

Example 4z4

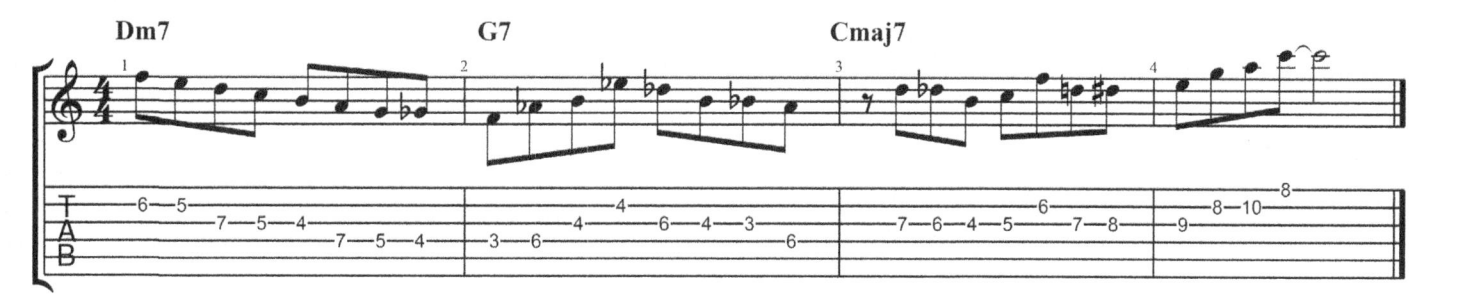

Here's the same concept applied again to create a brand new line.

Example 4z5

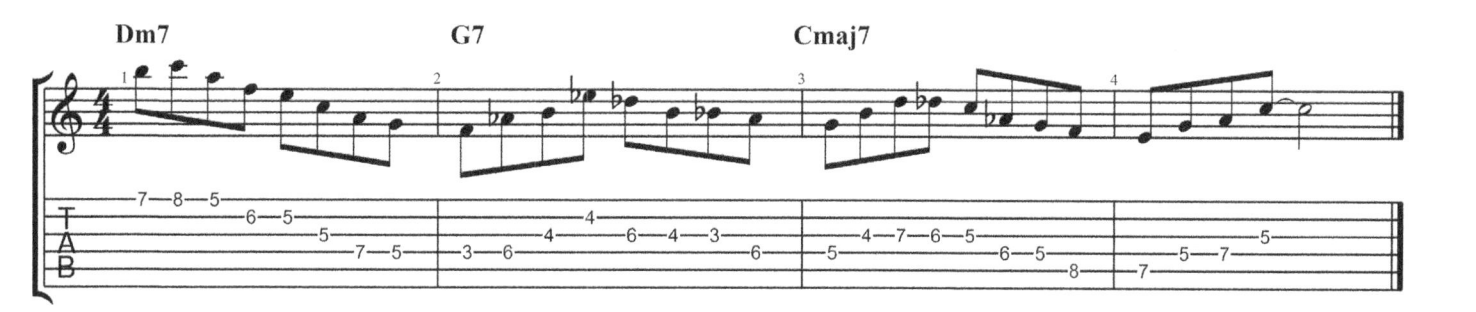

To end this section, here's another angular lick that uses an altered scale sequence in bar one and repeats the phrasing in bars 3-4.

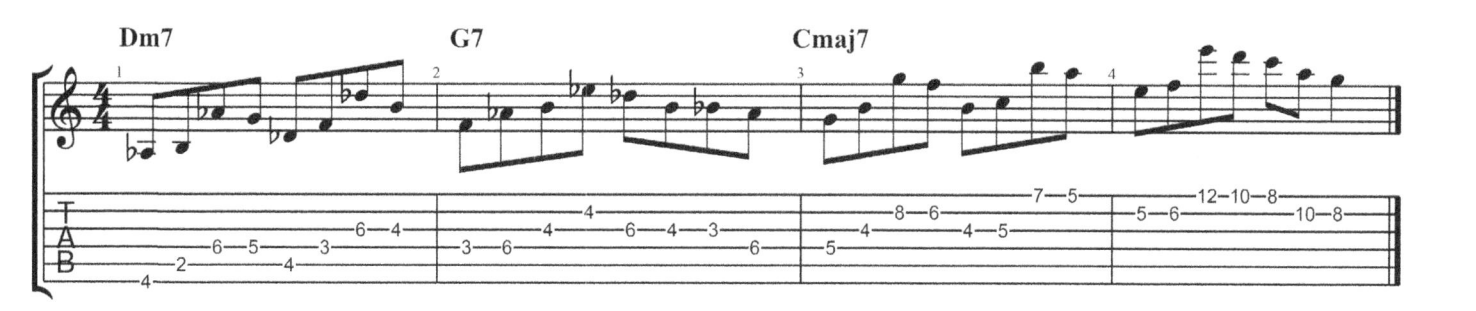

Example 4z6

Altered Scale Melodic Cells in a Minor ii V i

Now we're going to work through the process we've used throughout this book and apply altered scale cellular ideas to the minor ii V i progression (Dm7b5 – G7 – Cm7). We remember from the beginning of this chapter that the G Altered scale has no D note, so we begin that cell from the #5 (Eb) interval.

Let's define the minor cells.

Here is the dominant chord cell built from the G root note.

Example 4z7 – Minor Cell 1

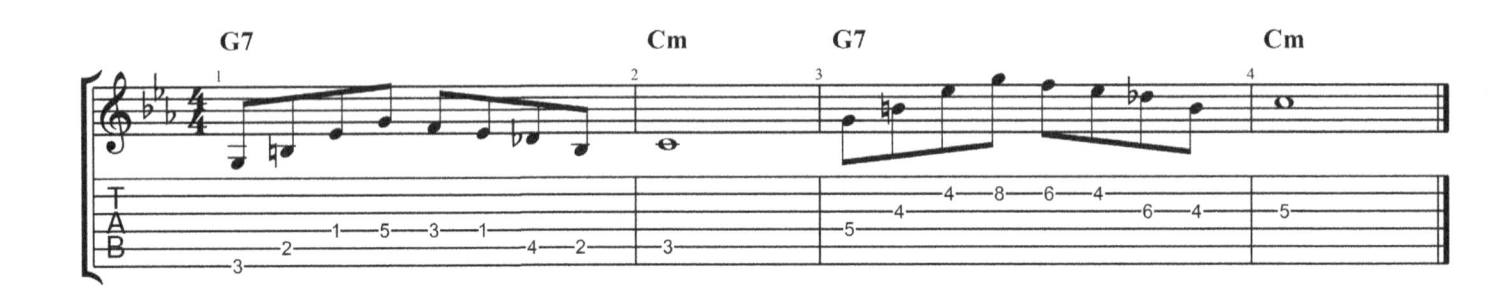

Next, Cell 2, built from the 3rd (B).

Example 4z8 – Minor Cell 2

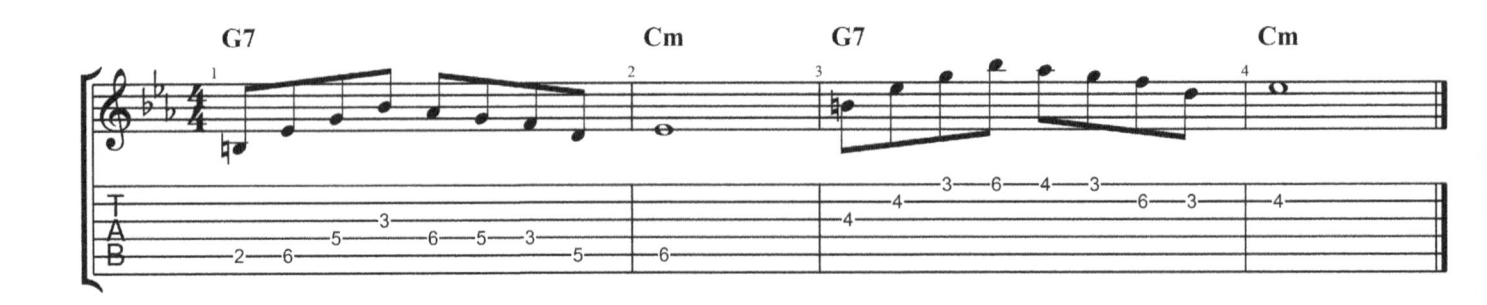

Here's the cell that launches from the #5 interval.

Example 4z9 – Minor Cell 3

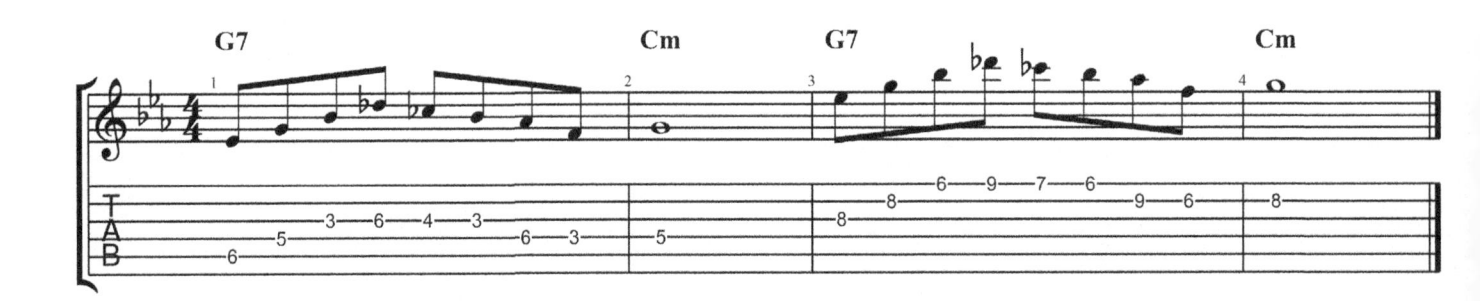

And Cell 4, from the b7 (F).

Example 4z10 – Minor Cell 4

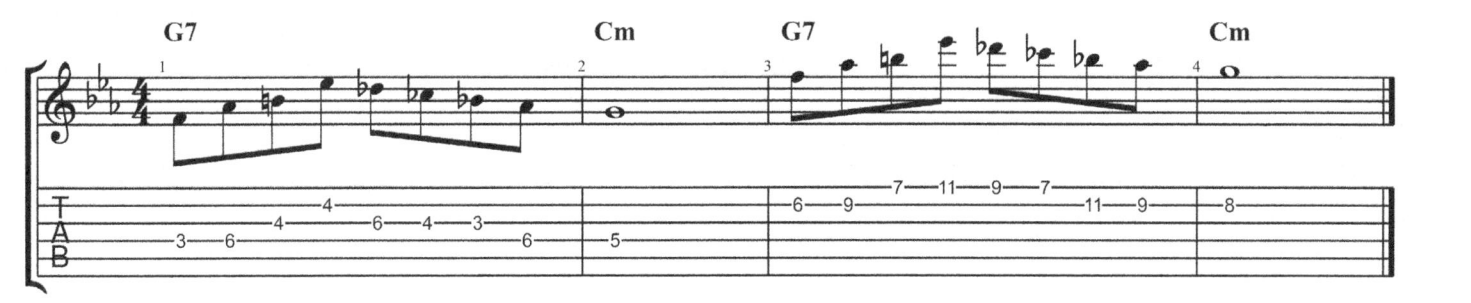

Putting the cells into a Minor ii V I

Obviously the cells are similar to the major cells seen earlier, with a small adjustment, but they sound completely different in the context of the minor ii V i sequence. Let's check that out by playing two simple lines for each cell.

Here are two lines for Cell 1.

Example 4z11

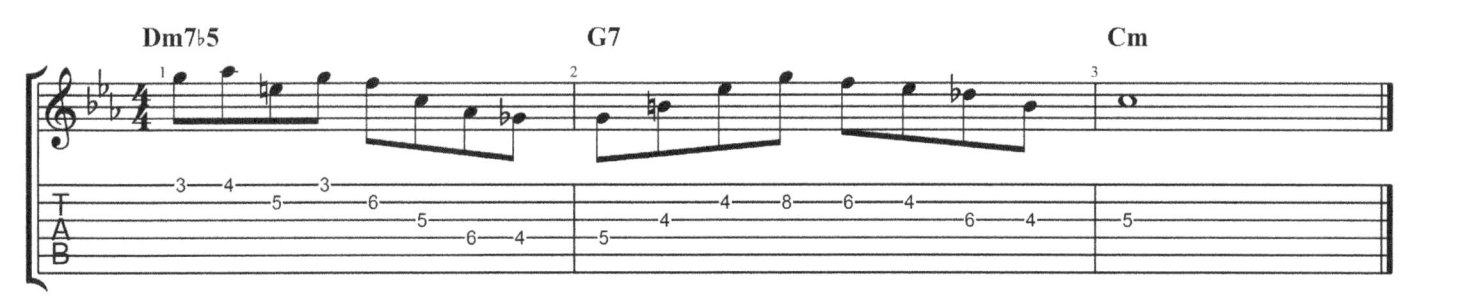

Example 4z12

Two lines that use Cell 2, from the 3rd.

Example 4z13

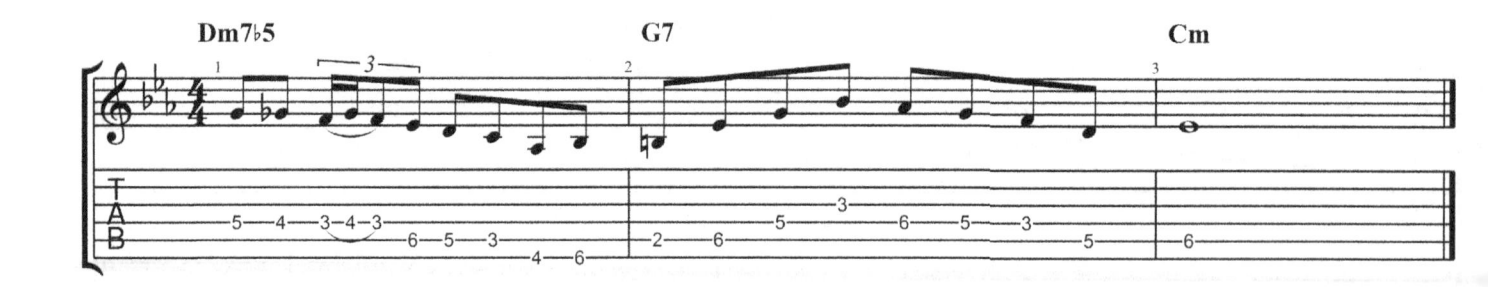

Example 4z14

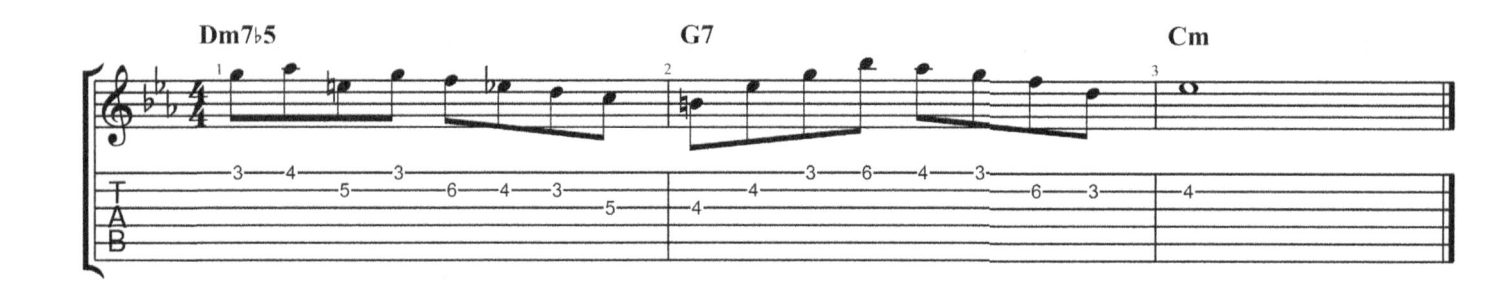

Next, two lines that use Cell 3, from the #5.

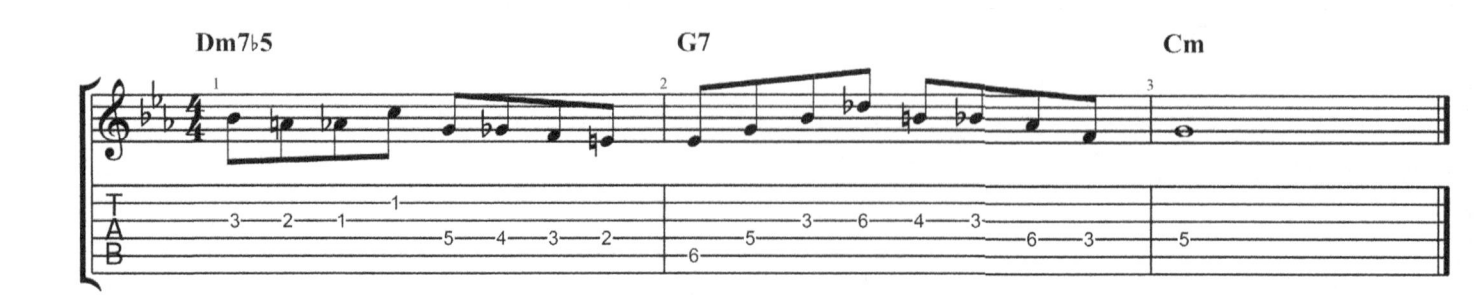

Example 4z15

Example 4z16

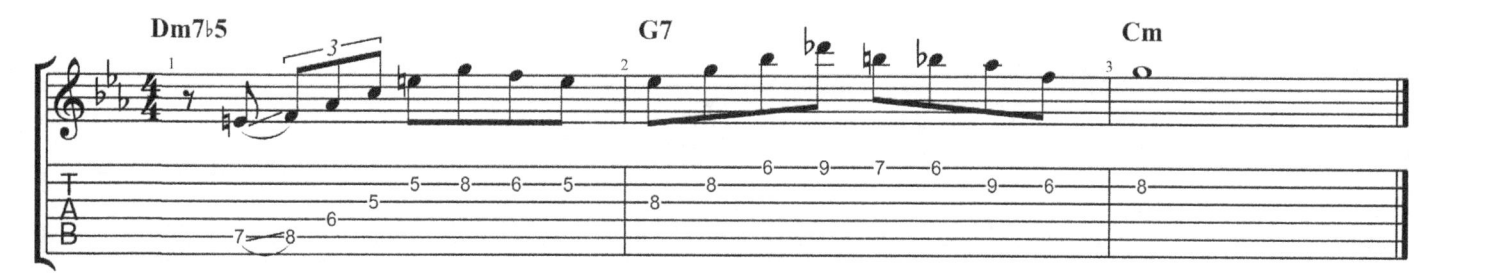

And, lastly, two lines that use Cell 4, from the b7.

Example 4z17

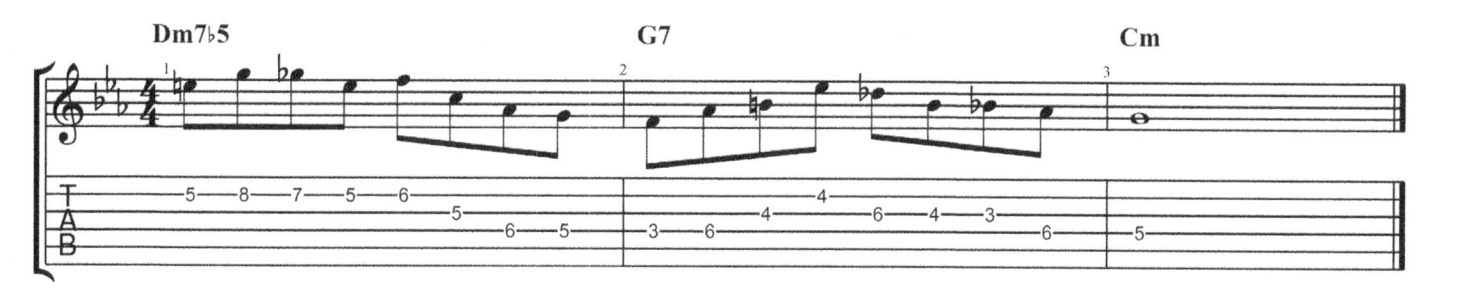

Example 4z18

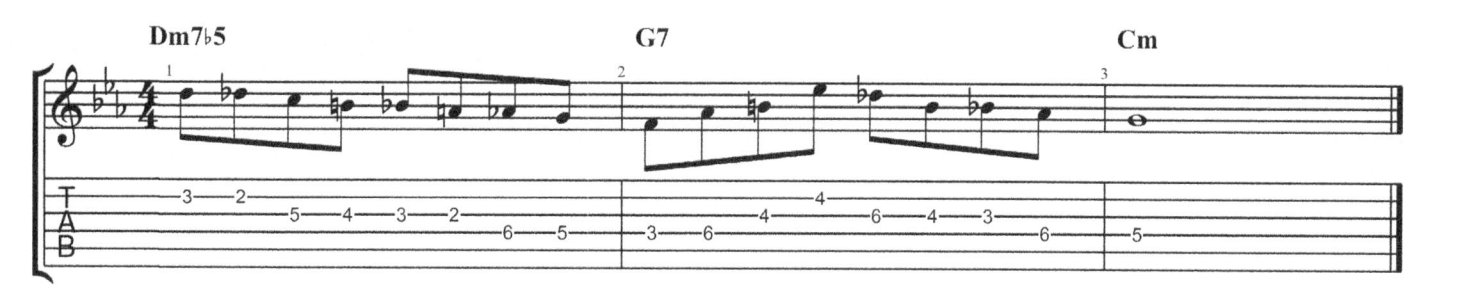

More advanced cellular vocabulary

With the stable core of every lick in place, let's see how these ideas can turn into some authentic licks. As always, we'll play five licks based on each of the four cells to complete our altered scale journey.

Though the key of C Minor contains an Eb, you'll have noticed that I often like to play an E note over the Dm7b5. Its effect is to create a richer Dm9b5 sound. The first part of this lick could therefore be seen as coming from the D Melodic Minor scale, but I think it's easier to think of it as a C Natural Minor scale with one note modified.

Example 4z19

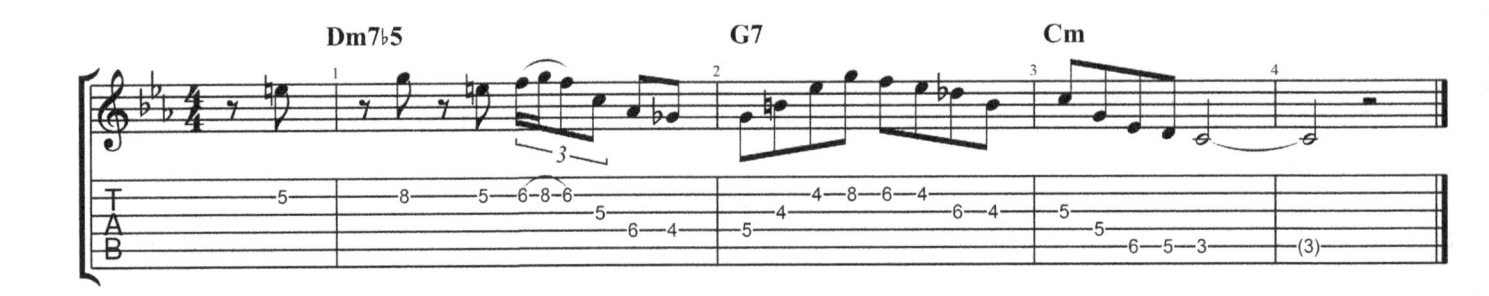

The next example contains a little substitution idea in bar one that you may not have thought of using. Look at the second group of four notes and play them as a chord (top note Ab on the first string 4th fret). You'll probably recognize this as an augmented chord. It comprises the notes Ab, E and C, then the Ab note is repeated.

You can move this shape around the fretboard in major 4th intervals (a distance of four frets) and each chord is an inversion of the original. So, this chord can be described as Ab augmented, E augmented or C augmented.

Like all chord substitution ideas, it works on the basis of common tones. Ab is the b5 of the Dm7b5 chord, C is the b7 and E is the 9th, as used in the previous example.

Notice that this 4th fret shape is located very close to the 5th position shape for Dm7b5 that you'd likely play if you saw it written on a lead sheet. Experiment with this idea, as you can create some cool licks by moving augmented shapes around the fretboard.

Example 4z20

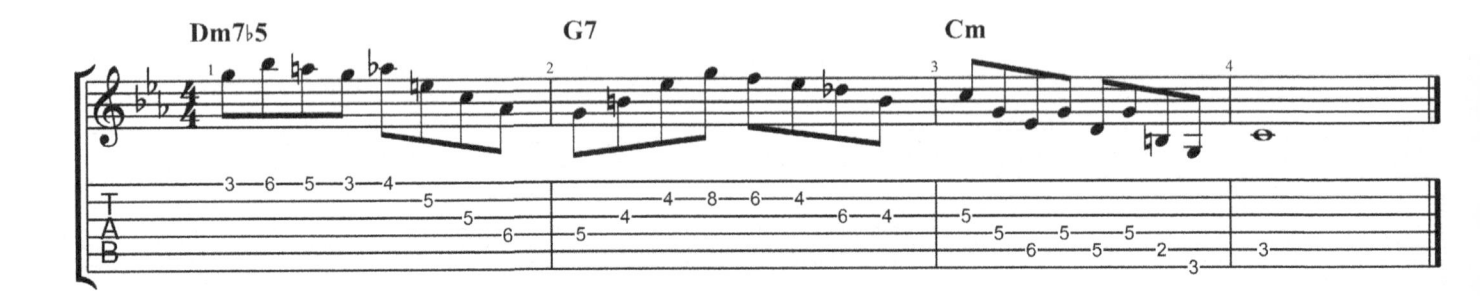

This next lick has an ascending run over the Dm7b5 chord. Study it and you'll see the Ab augmented triad embedded within it as part of the triplet phrase.

Example 4z21

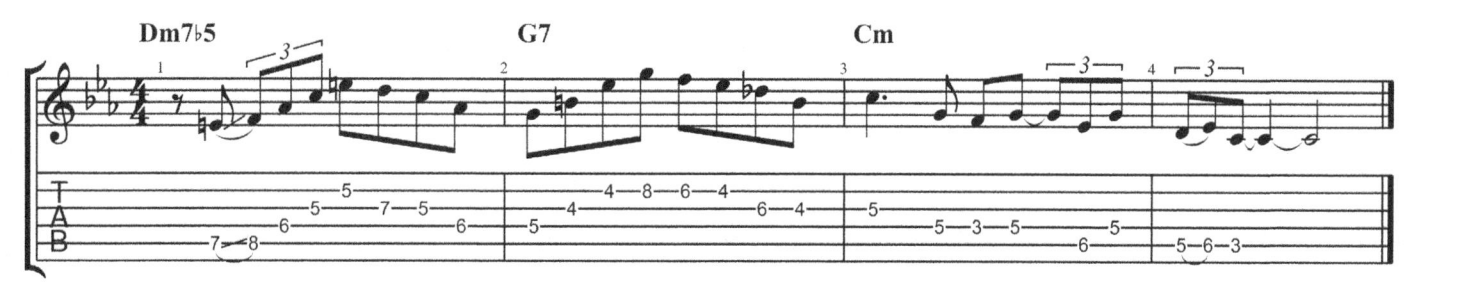

Here's a line that is broken up rhythmically. Listen to the audio first. Just looking at the dots, it can be tempting to play a line like this in a staccato manner, but you'll hear on the audio that the line still swings. It's a case of attacking the line with a swing mindset but gaining control over the rests without losing momentum. Play along with the audio to nail the feel.

Example 4z22

In Example 4z23 we're back to the C Natural Minor scale in bar one and a descending run that dovetails into the cell in bar two via a half step movement.

Example 4z23

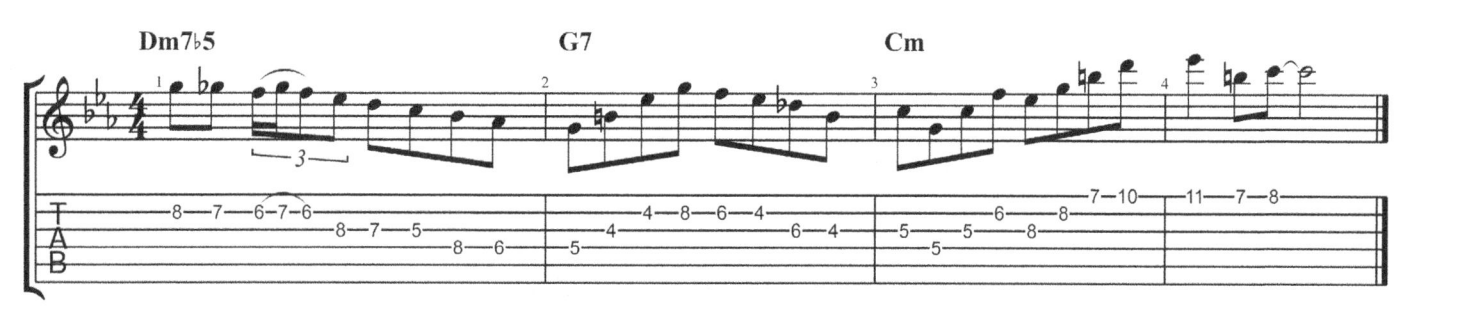

Now we turn to Cell 2, which begins on the 3rd (B) of G7.

This first idea utilizes the C Natural Minor scale in bar one and the second group of four notes spells out a Dm7b5 arpeggio minus the root.

Example 4z24

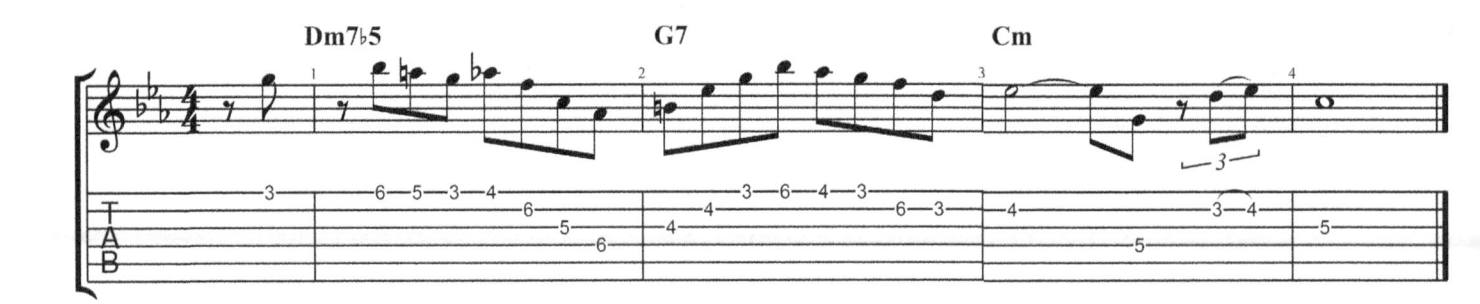

The next lick uses passing notes to build the phrase in bar one. The 1/8th notes of bars 1-2 are contrasted by a sparse phrase over Cm to end.

Example 4z25

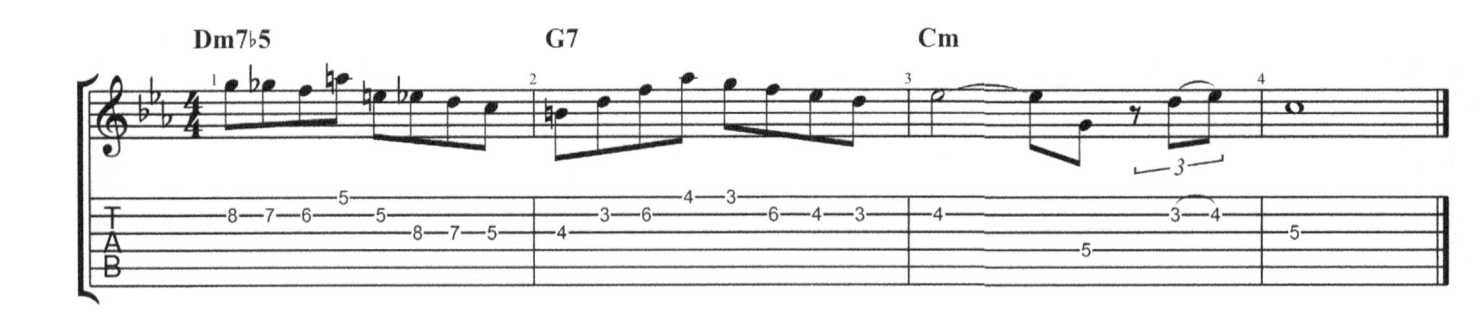

Next, here's a line that begins with the augmented lick of Example 4z21 but then heads in a different direction to connect with the higher register version of the cell.

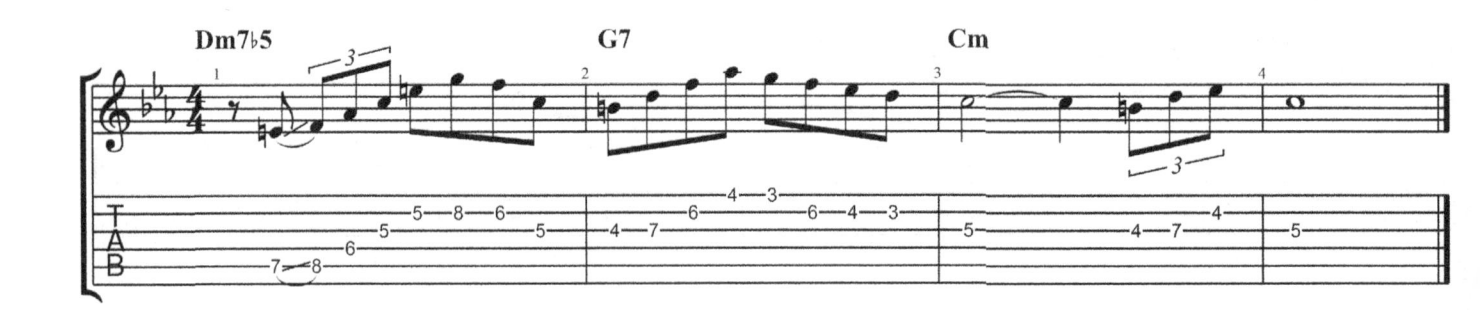

Example 4z26

In the next example, in bar one the same pattern of notes is played on the fourth and fifth strings. It's the C Natural Minor scale with added chromatic passing notes and creates a dark sound over the Dm7b5.

Example 4z27

Now for an outside sounding intervallic line to break away from straight 1/8th note passages. We're playing the G Altered scale over Dm7b5 and including some string skips. It's played at a reasonably swift tempo, so economic fingering and accurate picking are the order of the day here.

Example 4z28

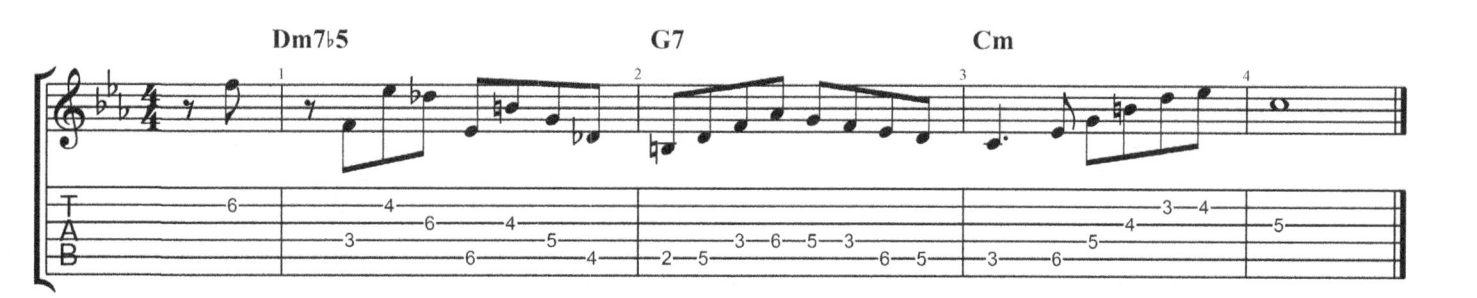

Next up are five lines using Cell 3, from the #5.

For this first example, the idea was simply to begin on the tonic note (C) and descend chromatically, with the first note of Cell 3 (Eb) as the target destination. Listen to the audio to get the articulation of the slurred phrase at the beginning.

Example 4z29

This is not a book about substitution ideas *per se*, but I'll pass on one more neat trick for you to explore here. When you encounter a minor 7b5 chord, you can play a harmonic minor scale over it whose root is a perfect 5th higher i.e. A Harmonic Minor over Dm7b5. A Harmonic Minor has the notes A B C D E F G#/Ab and the effect of superimposing it over Dm7b5 is to bring out some extended note colors. In the opening phrase, the B note is the 13th, the E is the 9th, and all the rest are chord tones.

Example 4z30

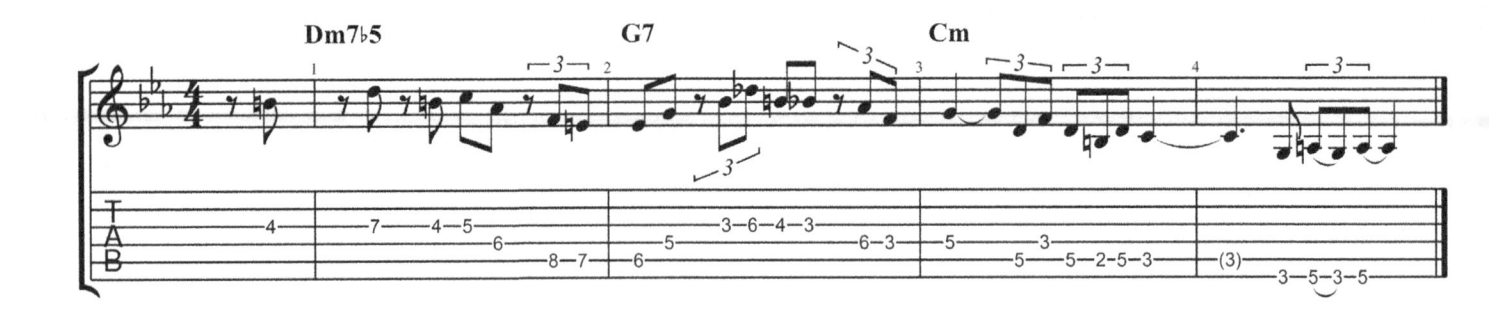

The idea for the phrase in bar one here was to approach Dm7b5 chord tones from a half step below.

Example 4z31

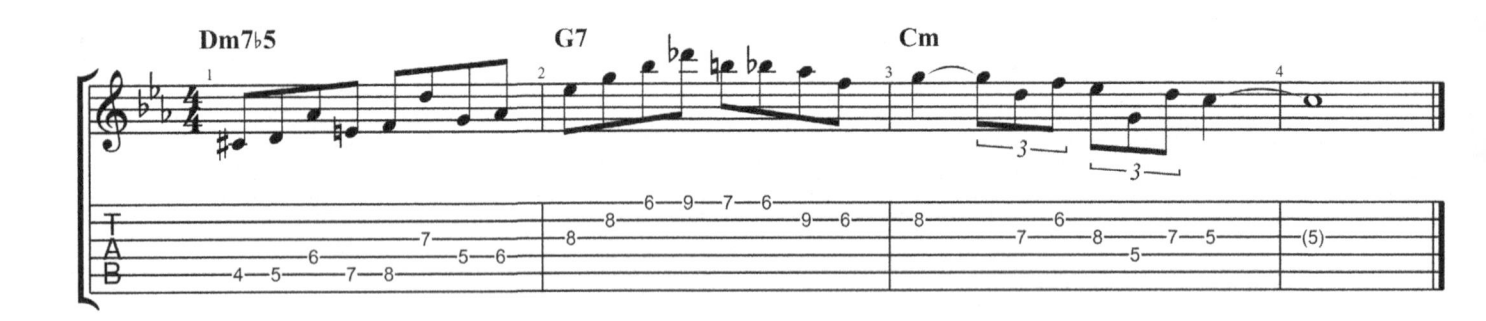

In Example 4z32, we begin the line with enclosures, where chromatic notes/scale tones surround target notes. The enclosure at the end of bar one crosses the bar line to target the Eb note of Cell 3.

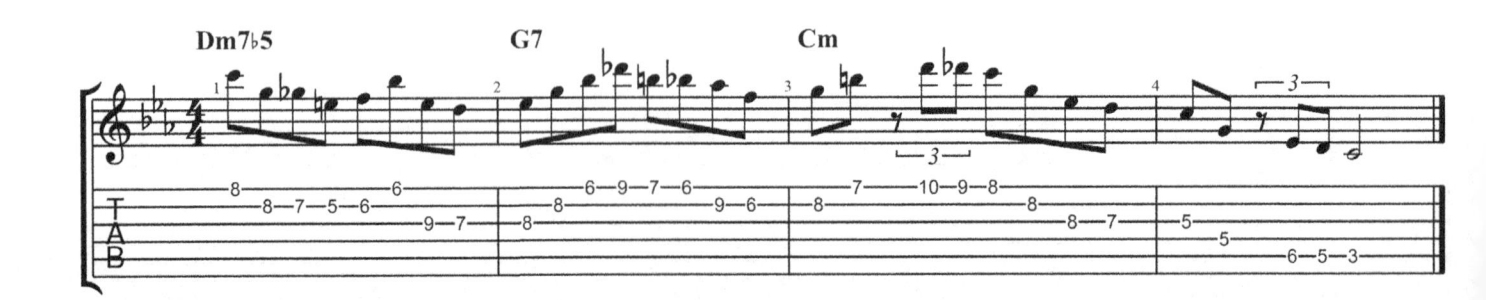

Example 4z32

Bar one of the next line returns to use the G Altered scale in an intervallic pattern, with the phrasing idea mirrored in bar three.

Example 4z33

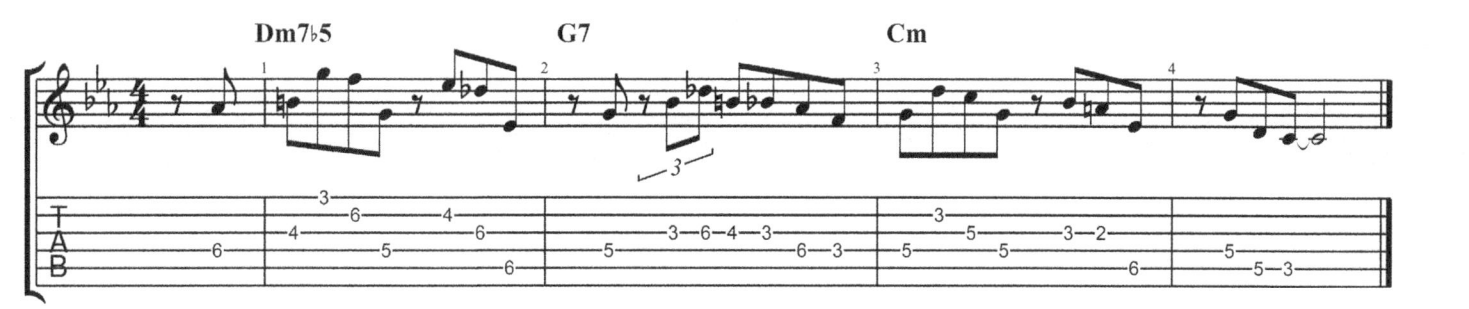

To close out this chapter, here are five ways of using Cell 4, from the b7 (F) of G7.

First, a simple run down the C Natural Minor scale with chromatic passing note transitions into our cellular phrase.

Example 4z34

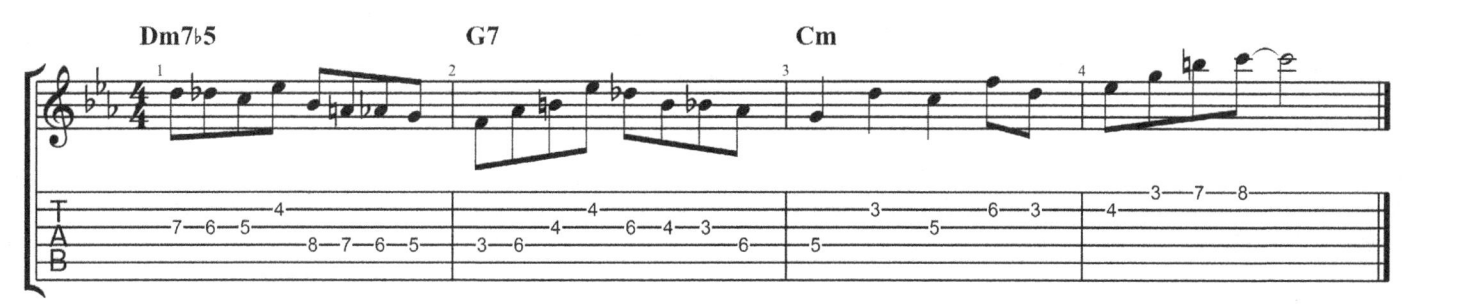

Here, another passing note phrase resolves up a half step to the higher register cell.

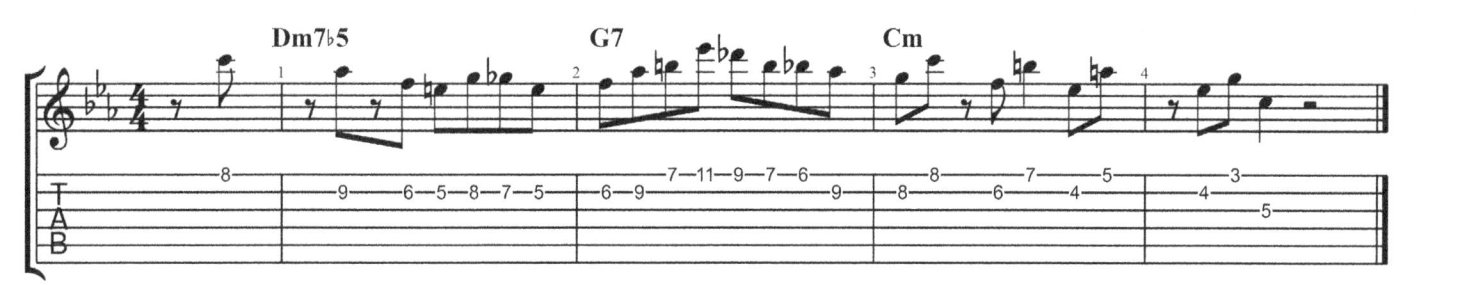

Example 4z35

C Natural Minor is used again in this phrase, where Db and B passing notes give the line an outside-inside feel. Over bars 3-4 we switch to the C Melodic Minor scale (C D Eb F G A B) for a different color.

Example 4z36

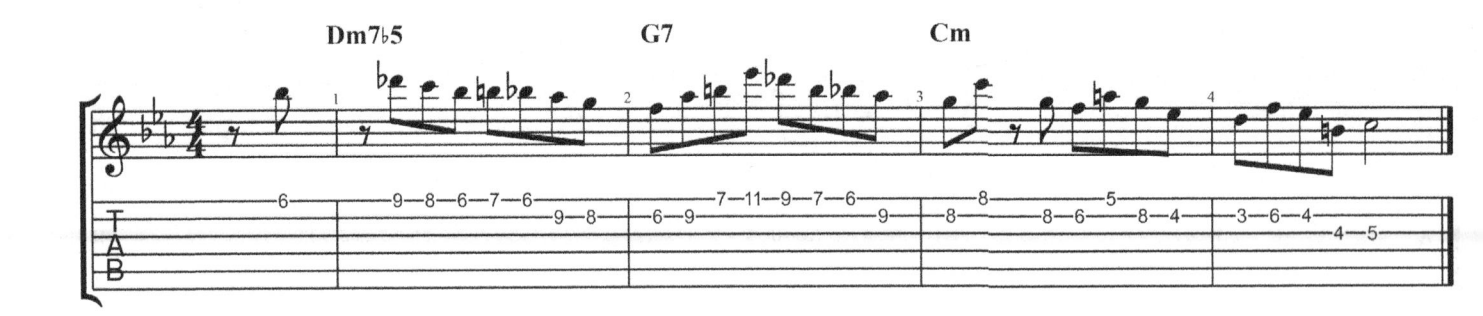

This line begins with a pedal tone idea that has an E note (the 9th of Dm7b5) at its center. The repeating pattern lick in bars 3-4 is a kind of hybrid of the C Natural and Melodic Minor scales. Here I was more interested in moving the pattern across string sets than specific note choices.

Example 4z37

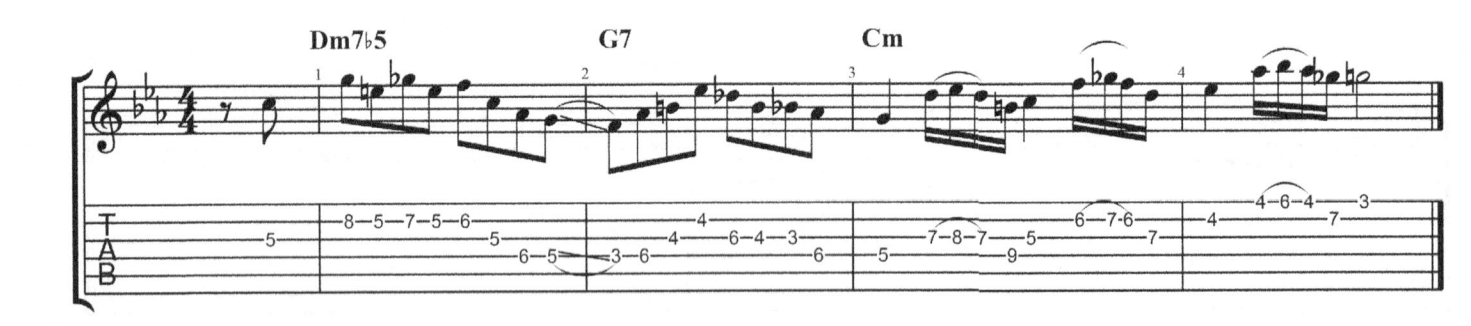

After altering the rhythm of the cell in bar two to disguise it a little, this line concludes with a C Melodic Minor run.

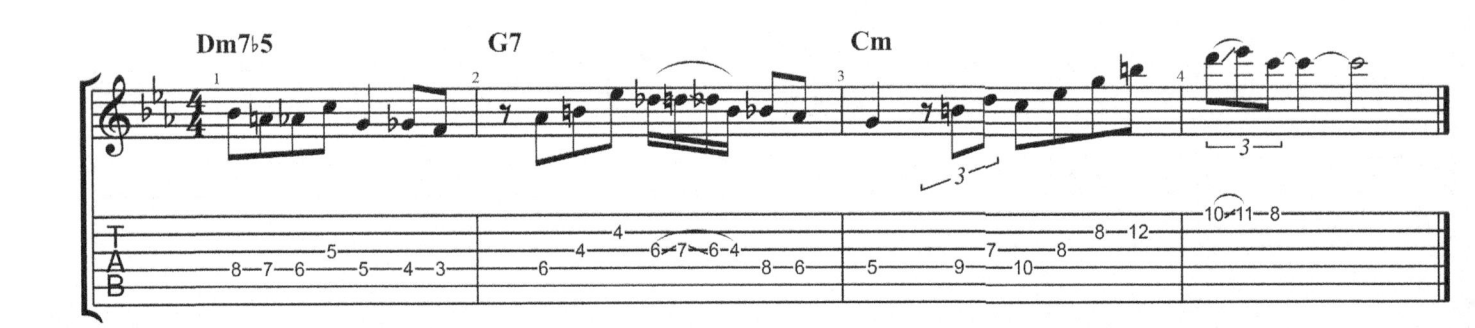

Example 4z38

Conclusion

I hope you've enjoyed this book. If you've worked through the material diligently, I'm sure you have added some cool new ideas to your jazz vocabulary. But more than that, I trust that applying this method – placing robust, well-formed cellular ideas at the heart of each line – has improved your phrasing and enabled you to play more succinct, musically satisfying ideas.

Don't stop here though!

Create some backing tracks for yourself, or find some on YouTube, revisit the core cells for each scale, and get practicing to create your own unique melodic ideas. I think you'll have a lot of fun and you'll definitely grow as a musician.

See you on road,

Oz.

Connect with me at:

https://www.oznoy.com

https://www.facebook.com/oznoymusic

https://www.instagram.com/oznoyguitar/

Made in the USA
Monee, IL
20 November 2022